LETTING GO LEADERSHIP

LETTING GO
LEADERSHIP

A Management Control
Model for Getting Results

DENNIS P. DRENT

ISBN:
Paperback - 978-1-7367988-2-9
Hardback - 978-1-7367988-0-5

Library of Congress Control Number: 2021907794

DEDICATION

This book is dedicated to my lifelong partner and wife, Susan. Any success I've had in achieving my dreams and ambitions would not have occurred without her support. I just hope she can say the same.

We must find time to stop and thank the people who make a difference in our lives.

——John F. Kennedy

Thank you for buying my book. I hope you enjoy it and gain some valuable insights. **Since translating ideas into action is never easy, I have provided a "Letting Go Leadership Control Model Template" at the end to help you take action.** Please visit my website at drentconsult.com to obtain your free Word version of this template to get you going!

Dachshunds are known to be fearless and stubborn with a strong streak of independence. If dogs were human, they might be our entrepreneurs. It is said a dachshund can learn anything it wants to.

Table of contents

INTRODUCTION

The purpose of a business is to create a customer.

—Peter Drucker

The world has many books on business. So, what does this one have to offer?

In a forty-year career, one is bound to learn something worth passing along. While this may be true for many people, I have had a unique set of experiences. I spent many years as a professional auditor before accepting CEO and COO roles at two entrepreneurial mid-market companies. As an auditor, I became knowledgeable about control—not just accounting controls but how to keep an entire company "in control."

But first, a little terminology:

"Control" is a verb where one is trying to direct or influence people's behavior or course of action. "Controls" is a plural noun and is the specific activities put in place to accomplish control. Control presumes you are trying to achieve specific objectives; for example, a business leader is trying to direct his employees' behavior so the business achieves financial success.

How leaders do this is critical. When companies are small, the founders can achieve control through personal involvement in every key decision. As companies grow and gain complexity, however, I have observed that too few executives understand the concept and power of control.

Being "in control" doesn't mean you are achieving your objectives. After all, factors outside your control may influence the results. But it does mean you know whether or not the objectives are being achieved. This enables an executive to make needed adjustments to achieve their objectives.

Control is important to ensure predictability. Predictability is necessary for organizational success. Investors want predictable returns, employees want their work environments to be predictable, and customers want a predictable experience. To be predictable, you must be in control. And being in control does not happen by chance.

Large public companies are typically in control. They are governed by securities laws and regulations that require them to be. I am always amazed at how accurately they forecast. However, it is very expensive to have the processes needed to keep a large company in control. It takes many highly paid accountants, financial analysts, HR professionals, sales analysts, lawyers, etc., to maintain this control. These companies also often fall into the trap of being over controlled. Their employees refer to this as bureaucracy.

Small companies can achieve control informally, typically, by having the CEO involved in every key decision. Of course, these companies are dependent on the quality of the CEO's judgment. Still, most founders have a vision for the company and do a good job maintaining early-stage control. The focal point of this book is what happens when a small, entrepreneurial company is successful and gets big.

Early-stage companies struggle for revenue and dream of the day they have a top line in the tens of millions of dollars. Oftentimes, when they get there, the expected profits don't follow. Management works just as hard and finds they are fighting one fire after another. The anticipated profits get eaten up by ever-increasing costs. Unless these companies are achieving a predicted profit shortfall or loss, they are not in control.

The problem is the company has outgrown the informal control structure of having the CEO make all the key decisions. The business becomes more complex, and some decisions would be better made by someone with more specific expertise. On the other hand, many decisions will linger waiting for the buried CEO to find time to focus on them. By the time they do, it is often a fire drill.

Companies that successfully transition from small- to mid-sized can flex into a more formal control structure. This is the idea of "Letting Go Leadership." The CEO learns to trust other people and the processes they create to keep things in control. This can be extremely difficult for the entrepreneur who has achieved so much success up to this point, trusting their instincts.

Entrepreneurs may scoff at the cost of the formal controls in this book, for example, upgrading the executive staff if necessary. The benefits are also hard to see immediately. This will be true for all the controls put in place. However, with time, the fire drills will recede and margins will increase, thus, realizing the long-anticipated profits. The key is to "right-size" the controls, for example, prioritizing and investing what you can afford over time. Results will start to improve with even partial implementation of the control model, particularly if they are effectively prioritized.

This book lays out a control model that I have used several times in my career to gain control over an organization. It works for any type of organization, including departments within large companies. So although this book was written with the entrepreneur in mind, it applies to any manager interested in achieving predictable results for their organization.

The concepts are universal across time and all organizations, and they are organized in an actionable manner. In my experience, people usually know what to do. Doing it is what differentiates winners from losers. And the world has room for an infinite number of winners!

My Story

I've spent my life working in businesses. I would have liked to have been an entrepreneur, but I didn't have the risk appetite it takes. Then, I graduated from college and got quickly hooked on a paycheck. I also liked the complexity of working for large companies as there were always interesting problems to solve.

Since big companies had the money to train people, I took full advantage of this and attended all kinds of seminars and read books, mostly about management and leadership. These companies wanted us to be good leaders on one hand but, on the other hand, didn't reward it. I was fascinated by the subject so just kept learning and hoping someday I would have the opportunity to use what I learned.

When I turned fifty, I was given the opportunity to run a specialty insurance company. The company had a good business model and should have been profitable. It wasn't. Every process in the company was broken. In my opinion, the founder had failed to understand that his leadership style of making every decision was holding the company back.

This was a unique opportunity to put everything I had learned to work. In about two years, we were making three times the return on equity as the average insurance company. People gave me credit for saving the company. But all I did was follow the concepts you will learn throughout this book. These concepts actually work.

During these two years of turnaround, I had numerous employees express concern about the company's viability. They were worried about their jobs. This became personal for me. I felt a responsibility for the employees and their families. I could never guarantee their jobs, but I could navigate the ship, so we didn't hit any icebergs.

I also learned about the impact we had on customers. You can imagine our customer service was not great given that every process was broken. I took many customer complaints to understand how we were doing. We sold pet insurance, which was hard to even take seriously for some people. However, pet owners bought our products, so they didn't have to choose between their pet's health and paying the cable or utility bill. And for many customers, our products were failing. I heard some sad stories.

Being responsible for employees and transparent to customers is all stuff found in the business books. I just took it seriously and put processes in place to deliver on our promises.

Changing Your Mindset on the Purpose of Business

Of the many books I read over the decades, I always came back to Peter Drucker. I read and reread his books to imprint his ideas in my brain. Drucker published *The Practice of Management* in 1954. I have sometimes thought nearly every business book written since has been a variation of this original thinking.

Drucker was a big-picture thinker and wrote about the critical role business plays in society. Most people believe that the purpose of a business is to make money. I certainly believed this. But Drucker taught me that the purpose of a business is to create a customer. It is the *responsibility* of the business to make a profit. If you can't make a profit, it means you don't have a product that adds value to society. Furthermore, without profits, you do not earn the right to stay in business.

Profitable businesses not only contribute by providing the products we need and want, but they also have the resources to contribute in general. For example, they pay taxes and support charitable contributions. In addition, their executives may participate in organizing community projects. Perhaps most importantly, successful businesses provide good jobs.

Most business executives and entrepreneurs don't read Peter Drucker. Too many people don't understand the potential for business to help solve many of our societal problems. In many circles, capitalism is a bad word. Ever since Karl Marx published *The Communist Manifesto* in 1848, capitalism has been under attack. And I can't say without good reason. Too many businesses only care about profits and don't care about workers or even customers.

Essentially, many entrepreneurs need to learn to balance the needs of the owners, employees, customers, and other constituents. They need to look beyond making money and see the critical role they play in society. They can first do this by ensuring they are optimizing their businesses through Letting Go Leadership.

CHECK-IN

Curiosity Defined the Weekend

Management by objective works—if you know the objectives. Ninety percent of the time you don't.

—Peter Drucker

The driveway pebbles crunched under the tires of the dark gray SUV as it slowly came to a stop. The entrance of the Great Desert Resort & Spa was enclosed by a patio misting system commonly used in the Phoenix area.

Tom and Susan Barrett live in Orange County, California, and make the trip to Scottsdale a few times a year. Having taken advantage of an infrequent weekend deal on this visit, they looked forward to enjoying the beautiful property and relaxing.

As Tom unloaded the bags, he noticed a man near the entrance standing just away from the mist talking on his phone. He could not hear what was being said, but the man looked concerned and appeared animated. Tom turned to Susan and whispered, "There's someone who may not be having a relaxing weekend." Susan told him to mind his own business.

While Susan checked in, Tom could not help but look back at the man on the phone. Instinctively, he knew this was a business call. Tom had spent forty years working as an executive and was winding down his career. And since Tom was pulled to solving business problems like metal to a magnet, he was dying to know what was going on.

Susan snapped Tom out of his daydream state and asked him to grab the bags. He did and followed her to the room. When they got to the door, the key card did not work. Tom quickly volunteered to go back to the lobby and get replacements. Back downstairs, he noticed the man on the phone was now inside.

Tom's curiosity was on overload at this point. Waiting for the keys to be made, he walked around as if taking in the beauty of the lobby while trying to hear some of the conversation. He heard the man repeat several times, "How could this happen?" Other than that, he heard some references to a credit agreement.

"Here are your room keys, Mr. Barrett. Sorry for the inconvenience."

"No worries; thanks for your help," Tom responded as he grasped the two new key cards.

Frustrated that he didn't catch more of the man's phone conversation, Tom headed back upstairs. The door opened to a large room that had a ceiling to floor window overlooking the golf course. The fairways were lush green. "I'm always amazed at how much it must cost to keep these golf courses in the desert so green," Tom said. "And seeing the courses always makes me wish I played."

"I hate golf!" Susan exclaimed.

"I know. I still think it would be something fun we could do together, but I know—not gonna happen."

"I think I'm going to find the pool and swim. What are you going to do?"

"I guess I'll go to the gym and stretch. By the time we both finish, it will be time to get ready for dinner. So, think about what you'd like to do."

Susan nodded. "OK."

Tom changed into a T-shirt and gym shorts while Susan changed into her swimsuit and headed out to find the pool. Tom did his typical procrastinating before heading to the gym.

THE GYM

The Problem is More Than a Weak Bench Press

We now accept the fact that learning is a lifelong process of keeping abreast of change. And the most pressing task is to teach people how to learn.

—Peter Drucker

Tom headed downstairs to find the gym and quickly looked around for the man on the phone. He was gone. *Good,* Tom thought, *maybe he's spending time with his family.*

Down the hall, he found a well-equipped fitness center with everything a fitness buff could hope for. Looking past the empty rows of shiny cardio equipment, he spotted the man from the lobby crouched on a bench in the free weights area. He was again on the phone and looked subdued. Tom watched him hang up.

As Tom rolled out a mat to begin stretching, he heard some grunting from the weight area. The man was on the bench press trying to press what looked like a substantial amount of weight. He got the bar above his chest and started to shake. He lost control and the bar slid to his right side.

Tom got up quickly and hurried over to help. Before he got there, the man used his left arm to push the bar up to protect it from slamming into him. The man was trapped under the bar but appeared to avoid getting hurt.

As Tom approached, the bar was lying on the man's chest, and he could not lift it to free himself. Tom pulled the weights off the man and asked him if he was all right.

Yeah sure, he replied. They always warn you to have a spotter, but I thought I could easily handle three hundred pounds. I pressed four-fifty in college. But anyway, thanks for your help. This place is empty, and I'm not sure how long I would have been trapped if you weren't around.

Glad to help. Tom chuckled. I always admired guys that could bench so much. I don't think I ever bench-pressed more than one-fifty.

The man stood up. Oh shit!

Are you all right?

Yes, yes, but the weights hit my phone and smashed it. I never let it out of my sight. Damn, not sure what I'm going to do. I guess I'll need to find an Apple store nearby.

Maybe you'll enjoy the weekend a little more without it? By the way, my name is Tom. Good to meet you.

Hi, Tom. My name is Ryan, very pleased to meet you.

Ryan, I'm going to be honest with you. When my wife and I were checking in, I noticed you were in a serious conversation on your phone. I don't want to be nosey, but it sounded like a business problem. You look very concerned about your phone. I spent a long career in management, and if there is something I can do, just ask.

What do you do?

All kinds of stuff, but I developed this niche expertise of helping companies make the transition from being small and entrepreneurial to professionally managed.

You mean take a nimble entrepreneurial company and turn it into a bureaucracy? Ryan asked sarcastically with a smile.

The men were now sitting on weightlifting benches facing each other. Tom had heard the sarcasm before when he talked with entrepreneurs about his vocation.

So, I assume you are an entrepreneur? Tom asked with a smile.

At least for a while. I need to get a new phone ASAP!

Would you mind telling me what's going on? You won't get a surprise bill, I promise.

Where would you like me to start?

I've got time. How about from the beginning?

Ryan gave Tom the following history of his business: Ryan graduated from Purdue University with a degree in biochemistry. He planned to become a veterinarian, but his grades were too low to get into vet school. After graduation, Ryan went to work for Big Pharma Inc. in Indiana as a veterinary pharmaceutical sales rep. It was a well-paying job that kept him close to the veterinary profession. He found his extroverted personality and a high appetite for risk were well suited for cold calling and winning new accounts. After a couple of years, he was doing very well financially.

However, Ryan found the big company environment stifling. He was always being written up for not submitting the proper paperwork on time and was frustrated that his ideas were ignored. His supervisors loved his sales results but found Ryan hard to deal with.

One day, Ryan was talking to a veterinarian client about a problem patient. It was a big dog that needed a unique mix of drugs that came in only one size pill. The veterinarian had to break the pills apart to give the dog what it needed. This took time and wasn't exact.

Ryan asked if this was common. It was; some local pharmacies would mix medications for veterinarians that needed a lot of drugs. These were called compound pharmacies. Ryan asked if he thought there was enough of this need to support a compound pharmacy dedicated to veterinarians. The vet wasn't sure but thought it was a good idea.

After asking many of his clients about his idea for a veterinary compound pharmacy, he concluded that there was a need, but the business would need to be large in scope to get the required volume to make it profitable. This would require logistical expertise in addition to pharmaceutical knowledge.

Ryan had saved enough money to quit working for six months and invest $60,000 into developing his idea. He teamed up with David, a logistics expert he had met at Big Pharma, and Ed, a local veterinarian and friend. David and Ed did not leave their jobs, but each contributed $10,000 and committed to ten hours of work per week.

Ryan formed a company called "National Veterinary Compound Pharmacy." He was issued 75 percent of the common stock and his two partners 12.5 percent each.

Ryan decided to start local and learn the pharmacy and logistics basics before expanding nationally. He hired a pharmacist on a part-time basis to mix the prescriptions in a small, rented warehouse. Ryan put together marketing and sales materials and helped Ed visit local veterinary hospitals to gain business. David worked on developing a process to deliver the completed prescriptions to the hospitals within twenty-four hours of filling the order.

The local business grew rapidly, and Ryan was able to raise an additional $100,000 from friends and family. He was careful not to dilute his ownership in the common stock.

David and Ed were working far more than ten hours per week, and the company was now generating positive cash flow. David and Ed left their jobs to fully invest themselves in the company. The heavy lifting of going national was ahead of them.

Building a national brand and infrastructure took years, but the company steadily grew and experienced no major hiccups. Although any veterinarian in the country could order compound medicines online, National's sales force was still limited to the Midwest. Ryan had plans to locate sales reps throughout the United States.

National was now seven years old and generating $30 million of annual sales. He had thought by the time he reached $30 million in revenue, the company would be very profitable. Yet despite these revenues, National struggled to achieve the cash flow needed to expand nationally.

About a year ago, the company borrowed $10 million from a non-bank cash flow lender to help fund its expansion. Ryan was confident the increased cash flow from expanding the business would quickly follow the investments and the debt would be paid off quickly.

Under the credit agreement, National needed to maintain a pretax profit of $2 million. It had achieved this level of profitability for the past two years.

So, I assume the $2 million is in jeopardy based on my nosey listening in on your phone call, Tom said.

I just can't believe it. My CFO called me and told me she was projecting a shortfall in income for this quarter's report to our creditor. If true, they'll be all over us. Penalties, fines, higher interest rates, sticking their nose in our business.

I'll be honest with you, Tom. It's not just the credit agreement. It seems like every day brings another surprise. One minute I'm bailing out the sales team who's having trouble closing a large veterinary hospital account, then I need to get involved to untangle a logistical jam. It's one thing after another. Sometimes I think nobody else knows how to get anything done!

What about your executive team?

Well, there's Allison, our CFO. I think she's solid, although I don't know how she could have missed this quarter's profitability projection if that turns out to be the case. She's very sharp and cut her teeth with a Big Four accounting firm.

Of course, my partner Ed is VP of sales, Ryan continued. He was good when we were small, and his job was solely calling on local veterinarians. He seems to be struggling with managing a small sales team and is lost when it comes to digital sales. He is also less comfortable calling on the expanding number of veterinary hospital chains.

My other partner, David, is VP of operations. He was a logistics guy at Big Pharma. His job is to ensure orders are received, processed, and delivered within the terms of our agreements with veterinary hospitals. He's doing an OK job but occasionally seems to disappear. However, he has a strong assistant that keeps things going when David is off the grid.

Carol is our Chief Veterinary Officer. It's her job to ensure the compounds are properly mixed, packaged, and ready to be shipped. Carol knows what's she's doing. She has a strong staff of well-trained professionals that understand the seriousness of their work. We have a zero-tolerance policy for errors.

We now have about fifty employees. So, we also have a small human resources department headed by an HR manager that reports to Allison. It's a pretty basic HR department that does primarily payroll, benefits, and keeps us legal.

Lastly, we have a marketing manager that technically reports to Ed, but Carol and I provide a lot of input here. I have a feel for the brand message we want to send, and Carol knows how to communicate with veterinarians.

I have formed an operating committee that includes my direct reports, plus Becky and Erin. Becky is our HR manager and Erin our marketing manager. We meet once a month. Allison plans the meeting and tracks the action items. However, I don't feel like this meeting is as effective as it needs to be. We tend to discuss the same things each month and key items take forever to get done.

Tom put up his hand. Let me summarize. You started National about seven years ago, and the company has grown from zero to $30 million in revenue. About a year ago, you borrowed $10 million for a national expansion you originally thought would be funded through cash flow. The credit agreement requires you to maintain a pretax profit of $2 million, and Allison is saying you may not meet that requirement this quarter. Despite her previous projections indicating you would.

You are personally working hard to perform duties that you believe your executives should be doing, like closing a large hospital group new sale. You have serious reservations about Ed's ability to grow with his job, and David goes off the grid from time to time. These are your two partners that together own about 25 percent of the company. Am I close?

That's not a bad summary, Ryan responded.

At that moment, a boy entered the gym holding a phone out toward Ryan. Dad, he said, it's Allie at work. She couldn't reach you, so she called Mom.

Ryan reached out to grab the phone. Hi, Allie, is everything all right? Don't worry about it, Ryan continued. We all make mistakes and things have been crazy. We'll make it up, we'll get through it. No, don't say things you don't mean.

Allie, we need you. I need you. Why don't you take the weekend off, and let's talk about this on Monday after a couple of nights' sleep?

OK, get some rest and take care. We'll talk Monday.

That didn't sound good, Tom said.

I forgot to tell you Allie is pregnant and has become pretty good friends with my wife. She feels so bad about this profit shortfall she wants to resign. Losing Allie right now would be a disaster!

Ryan, I need to meet my wife in a few minutes. Would you be able to continue this conversation after dinner, say at nine at the bar? Tom asked. I have some things to share that may help.

You certainly have my curiosity, and I think given the situation, my wife would agree to any help I can get. I'll see you at nine.

THE BAR

Working All the Muscles

No institution can possibly survive if it needs geniuses or supermen to manage it. It must be organized in such a way as to be able to get along under a leadership composed of average human beings.

—Peter Drucker

The bar was modern looking with liquor bottles stacked five shelves high in front of mirrored panels. Lights of various colors reflected off the mirrors and bottles, providing a stimulating atmosphere. Citrus fragrance permeated the room.

Tom walked in and saw Ryan sitting on a black leather stool at the end of the bar.

Hey, Ryan, Tom called out over the crowd.

Ryan waved him over.

What do you have? I'm buying, said Ryan.

Oh, I think I'll have a Rob Roy tonight. Thanks!

Ryan ordered a Rob Roy for Tom and a Jack Daniels neat for himself.

Any word from Allison? Tom asked.

First, I have good news. I was able to find an Apple store and replace my phone! So Allie and I have traded a few texts. I think she's off the cliff, but I don't think I'm home free. I've got work to do there, Ryan responded.

You know, I was thinking. I think there's an analogy in how you work out and run your business.

Really?

I assume you like bench pressing because your shoulders are your strongest muscles, and you get positive reinforcement from lifting heavy weights? Tom asked.

Never thought about it, but I suppose that's right.

We all have strengths that give us the success we have. But we tend to overuse those strengths and ignore other ones we need to maintain that success or even increase it. I suspect your greatest strength is you get stuff done; that's your business equivalent of the bench press.

I love getting shit done.

That's a great attribute to have, and I wish more people had it. But if you only use this strength, what happens? Tom asked.

Ryan thought for a moment. I could end up doing other people's work for them.

Exactly! This is the equivalent of having super strong shoulders but weak back, leg, and stomach muscles. This does not make for a healthy body! At some point, these weaker muscles are going to hold you back. Also, you are likely to hurt yourself overworking your shoulders, like you almost did today!

A few years ago, I noticed I was getting body pains that I never had before. It comes with aging, Tom said. I was watching PBS one night and saw this program on stretching. The woman made the point that you don't need to work any one muscle hard, but you need to work every muscle a little bit a few times a week to stay in shape. She, of course, had a program that you could buy that would help you do this.

I suppose you bought it, said Ryan.

I did, and it has been like magic. I feel great—most of the time!

Your mind is no different than your body. You must work different mental muscles to stay in shape. And since you are the leader of National, if you're not using all your mental muscles, the business will suffer as a result. There is a reason CEOs are paid so highly: they have a powerful and unique influence on the business.

So how do you know what to do? There's no corpus of your mental muscles. They don't start hurting when you don't use them.

That's right—you need a map.

My guess is you have one, Ryan said.

Well, there are thousands of business books that provide great advice. Some are written by business school professors grounded in theory and others by successful business practitioners. I have my ideas based on experience, which I'm happy to share with you. Keep in mind this will be a high-level map. Business is complex and there are no silver bullets. Each topic would require a full book to thoroughly explore, but maybe I can get you pointed in the right direction.

I'm all ears!

I'm going to start with a broad framework, and we can drill into the specific areas of focus. I'll use some acronyms to help jog your memory. The first acronym is PCP. No, we are not talking about angel dust. But if that helps you remember the acronym, great.

PCP stands for People—Community—Process. These are the major muscle groups of your business. There's not enough that can be said about having the right people. Every company claims it has the best people. This may seem impossible, but maybe it's not. Maybe they have the best people for what they need. Even companies in the same business have different cultures that require certain types of people.

The key is to match the people to the needs of the business. When you think about it, everyone is a composite of skills, knowledge, experience, relationships, and talent. That's the second acronym—SKERT. Skills. Knowledge. Experience. Relationships. Talent.

Sounds like this could be another one of those books you mentioned? Ryan said.

Absolutely, Tom responded. And there are plenty out there. We won't have time tonight, but I'd be happy to dig into this in a little more detail later.

That would be great.

A company needs to be deliberate in attracting, developing, and retaining the right people that have attributes that are most relevant to the company. Of course, having the right people is not enough. Even the best people will be ineffective if they are scattered and running in different directions. It is the leader's job to get them all pulling in the same direction. Like that common image of a rowing team. And that brings us to the C in our acronym: **Community**. Once you've got your people, you need to build a community of people who have a common purpose and are aligned in creating something bigger than themselves. This is where PVS comes in, our next acronym; that stands for Purpose, Values, and Strategy.

I have often asked people what the purpose of a business is. The most common answer I get back is to make money. This is the biggest misconception of capitalism. I think it helps create a backlash against capitalism today.

Peter Drucker wrote decades ago that the purpose of a business is to create customers. Who am I to judge, but I think he was a hundred percent right. Without customers, there is no business. There is no value created for anybody.

Most successful businesses have a clear purpose. You are in the animal health business so you will understand my example. I was once involved with a pet health insurance company whose purpose was to take the financial aspects of deciding how to medically treat pets out of the equation. In other words, to allow pet owners to solely focus on optimal medical treatment for their pets regardless of cost. This company had hundreds of employees who were passionate about this purpose. They were all animal lovers and bothered by the fact that any pet owner would have to sacrifice the best medical treatment for financial considerations.

I believe that purpose must be supplemented by a vision. The vision takes the purpose to a more aspirational level. One of my favorite vision statements was the original Microsoft vision of "A computer on every desk and in every home."

So, it's one thing to have the right people. But those people must be aligned with a purpose beyond making a living. They need a vision for what they want to accomplish. This empowers them to make day-to-day decisions that move the business forward.

The V in PVS stands for Values. Common values are needed so that people can work effectively together. Think about it. If you value integrity, you will meet your commitments to me. But if I don't meet my commitments to you, how well will we work together over time? This is critical for the CEO or leader of any organization to understand. Your values will be emulated whether you know it or not.

I worked with one organization that was focused on its customers. But underneath, the owners were primarily concerned with making lots of money to feed their lavish lifestyles. It felt like chaos. Employees were always pushing for more and more compensation. There wasn't much teamwork—it was a "me" culture. The pet health insurance company I talked about before had four common values: Passion. Integrity. Respect. Courage. The CEO talked about these values tirelessly. Most importantly, he demonstrated them. Because of this, there was a tremendous amount of loyalty to the company and people worked together to achieve its purpose and vision. And by the way, it made lots of money.

The S in PVS stands for Strategy. A strategy is needed to provide clear direction on what needs to be done to achieve the purpose and vision. Thousands of books have been written on strategy. There's something sexy about it, and most people want to be involved in it.

I boil strategy down to three things:

1. Setting your goals and desired future state,
2. Assessing where you are (current state), and
3. Creating a set of steps to get you from where you are (current state) to the goals and desired future state.

All three of these steps are critical and difficult. To make it even harder, a good strategic planning process will likely come up with more action steps than can be done realistically. You must, therefore, prioritize and match actions to resources. And I can assure you there will be strong differences of opinion on your management team as to what's most important!

I'm sorry, Ryan. I've been babbling for a while now. Have I lost you?

It's a lot to take in, Ryan said. I think I'm with you, though. Let me put it in my words. The analogy you started with is working every muscle. If you overuse your strongest muscle and ignore other muscles, you not only risk hurting your strongest muscle, but underworked muscles will weaken. Causing all kinds of things to go wrong.

The three muscle groups for running a business are PCP: People. Community. Process.

Getting the right people is a matter of knowing what skills, knowledge, experience, relationships, and talents you need. Then find the best people with those attributes.

Once you have the right people, you need to build a community with PVS. Having a common purpose and values gets everyone rowing together. Wrapping a strategy around the purpose and values provides common goals and agreed-upon steps to achieve them. It's like you now have the right people doing the right things the right way!

That's a great way of putting it, said Tom. There is one more muscle group to discuss: the second P for Process.

In addition to knowing the company purpose, vision, and strategic direction, people need to know what to do at a detailed level. Everything comes down to work. And work is done through processes, Tom said.

Any organization is a summation of its processes. Processes move things forward in an organized way. This is where the concept of control really comes in.

Let me ask you, Ryan. How do you control National?

I'm a control freak, Tom. You must have figured that out by now. I control things by staying involved in everything.

This is your bench press. You make sure stuff gets done by being involved in every detail of the business. And how is that going? Tom asked.

Well, I feel in control. That's a good feeling. However, I continue to get negative surprises, and despite growing revenues to $30 million, we can't sustain the profitability we need to grow and maybe even service debt.

OK, before I get to that, let's spend a minute talking about the concept of control. I believe control is only meaningful if it relates to an objective. Think about all the controls built into driving a car. Both the controls in the car and the rules of the road. These are designed to achieve the objective of safety. Control is, therefore, achieved when you have predictability. I know if I use the tools built into my car to follow the rules of the road, I can predict when I will safely arrive at a destination point. This, of course, assumes no unanticipated traffic jam. This same concept applies to every business process.

Many entrepreneurs need to feel in control. They are typically self-confident individuals and have a clear vision of what they are trying to achieve. They trust themselves and lack that same level of trust in others. They will, therefore, micromanage people so that there are no mistakes.

When a business is in start-up mode or it's still small, micromanaging can work. One person can effectively oversee a dozen people. Of course, these people need to be competent in their tasks. They're just not allowed to make any judgments or key decisions.

When a company successfully grows, like National, this control model breaks down. Back to the car analogy. Think about what would happen if you didn't trust your car's speedometer, so you took a stopwatch with you every time you drove, constantly checking your speed manually. This would increase your likeliness of speeding or even getting into an accident from the distraction.

Ryan jumped in. I assume you're suggesting the issues I'm having at National are of my own making. That by being involved in every decision, I'm using a stopwatch to make sure the speedometer is working?

I've got to believe at least some of them are, but I don't know, said Tom. Let me ask this—are you happy with the way things are at National, or do you think some change is needed?

I think we need a lot of changes. There are too many surprises, and we are not getting the consistent profitability needed to fund our growth or even service our debt.

OK. May I suggest the first thing that needs to change is . . . you?

Ouch, said Ryan. So, I was right. You're saying National's issues are of my own making.

That's a deeper conversation, but let's get back to the Process muscle group.

I've been around companies of all sizes, and the leaders of these companies have one thing in common: they think processes are too detailed for executives to bother with. Unfortunately, this attitude can lead to an abdication of responsibility for processes. Keep in mind abdication is different from delegation. When you delegate, you are entrusting someone else to do a task, but you maintain responsibility. Abdication is disowning something and essentially walking away from any responsibility. Processes can and should be delegated to competent middle managers. But any executive that abdicates responsibility for processes is in for trouble.

A company is a summation of its processes. Each process has objectives that support the business. For example, one objective of the sales process is to generate the desired revenue and gross margin from the products the company offers. However, the sales process cannot stand alone. It is impacted by other processes, such as marketing, customer service, human resources, finance, etc. Each of these processes also has objectives that must be achieved for the whole to work.

Control is not about the CEO making every decision. Control is the CEO knowing the status of every key process in meeting their objectives. And corrective action must be taken any time a key process is failing to meet its objectives.

Also, any innovation or business improvement must flow through a process. I like to say ideas are cheap and implementation is everything. Ideas are implemented through processes. So, if processes are meeting their current objectives but the results are not good enough, the objectives must be strengthened. Of course, the process must then be changed somehow to meet those higher objectives.

This is where you need to unleash the creativity of the people that own the processes. When a CEO is making every decision, this can't happen, and things start to fall apart. Does this make sense? Tom asked.

It does. I can see the need for this as a company grows. But you've got to have the right people. I'm concerned if I start letting other people run our processes without my input, things will start to fall apart. I don't know if that's because they aren't capable or just don't care.

I'm particularly concerned about my partners. You would think as owners they would care. I think Ed does care, but he's in over his head. On the other hand, David seems up to the job, but he's lost his passion for the business.

Yes, said Tom, you need to work all the muscles, and people are sort of like your back muscles. It's hard to work any muscle group if your back is hurting. You need to get this right before anything else. And it sounds like you have some big issues between Allison's wanting to check out and your partners.

It's getting late. Maybe we should call it a night but continue in the morning over a cup of coffee? We can do a deeper dive into Ed, David, and Allison and talk about your people in general.

OK, I need to get back up to the room. I promised my son we'd watch a movie. How about meeting at the coffee shop at eight? Ryan asked.

Perfect. See you there. Enjoy the rest of your evening.

The two men got up from the bar and walked in opposite directions to get to their respective rooms.

COFFEE

People, It's All in the Beans

Executives owe it to the organization and to their fellow workers not to tolerate nonperforming individuals in important jobs.

—Peter Drucker

As Tom approached the coffee shop at eight o'clock sharp, Ryan was sitting at a wooden table near the window and waved him over. Tom noticed the baristas were busy. In addition to the sounds of grinding coffee and the smell of frying bacon, Tom noticed the cheerful demeanor of the restaurant. Nearly every table was full of people that looked to be enjoying the morning.

Good morning, Tom. Have a seat. I'm eager to have this conversation.

Tom noticed that Ryan had not yet ordered anything. You a coffee drinker? Tom asked.

Absolutely. I was just waiting for you.

The server approached the table. She was young and full of good cheer. What can I get for you gentlemen? she asked with a big smile.

Tom responded, I noticed some tables have French presses. Can we get two French press coffees?

Sure, I'll be right back with them. Would you like blonde or dark roast?

Dark roast. Thanks for asking, Tom responded.

French press? Ryan questioned.

It's the best way to make coffee. The coffee and hot water just sit in the press for a few minutes without dripping through a paper filter. And since the filter absorbs some of the coffee flavor and oils, with a French press, you get all the flavor. No filtering. Most people probably wouldn't notice the difference, but I take my coffee seriously!

Speaking of coffee, what do you think is the most important thing about making good coffee?

Never gave it much thought.

The beans, Tom said. It's all about the beans.

But there are all kinds of different beans, from dark to light roast and various aromas and flavors from all over the world. Coffee is a fruit, and like any fruit, it can taste different depending on where it is grown. Look at how different varieties of apples taste. With coffee, you need to explore to find your favorite blend.

People are kind of like this as well. We all have some common attributes that tie us together as humans. However, there are many varieties of people, and we are all suited to do different things. This must certainly be by design. Think what the world would be like if we didn't have engineers or artists.

But just like an individual has a unique taste for coffee and must find the right beans, a company has a unique need for talent and must find the right people. Coffee connoisseurs may find coffee beans complex, but they are nothing in complexity compared to us humans.

To simplify the complexity of human beings, the capabilities of any employee can be broken down into five qualities. As I mentioned in the gym, I use the acronym SKERT. Skills. Knowledge. Experience. Relationships. Talent.

Skills are the expertise needed to do a task. For example, an accountant needs to have the skills of closing the books to create a monthly financial report. Skills are developed through a mix of gaining knowledge and experience.

Knowledge is having the theoretical or practical understanding of a subject. In your business, the pharmacists mixing the compounds require extensive knowledge of medicinal drugs for use in animals and sale.

Experience is the practical knowledge or wisdom you gain from what you have observed, encountered, or undergone. This is a real-world test. For example, a lot of marketing ideas look great on paper and may even test well. But good marketers have a sense of the marketplace from having tried different things over time. It's an instinct gained from experience.

We don't always think of **relationships** as part of a person's capabilities even though they are perhaps the most important. There is a reason the adage "It's not what you know, it's who you know" continues to be as relevant today as ever. Having the right contacts opens doors to getting things done. This is obviously true in sales but also in raising capital, overcoming regulatory hurdles, or simply having access to needed expertise.

Talent is a catch-all capability that essentially describes what we are good at. Although the list is long, some of the characteristics of talent include IQ, disposition, energy level, extroversion, creativity, logic, empathy, self-awareness, expression, etc. These capabilities are hardwired into our brains and bodies, and we can't do much to improve them.

Why don't we do a quick assessment of the skills, knowledge, experience, relationships, and talent of your key executives?

Ryan said, That would be great if it doesn't take too long.

We can do a high-level assessment. A more in-depth analysis would need to be performed with a professional coach before making any big decisions.

Let's start with your CFO, Allison. What skills do you need in a CFO at National?

She needs a combination of accounting and financial analysis skills. Our CFO closes the books, compiles and analyzes the financial statements, and completes and files all the reports with our creditor, the IRS, and other regulatory agencies. She also has a staff, so she needs to have the skills required to motivate people in getting stuff done in a somewhat chaotic environment.

That's a good list, said Tom. Would you say Allison is proficient in those skills?

No doubt.

What about knowledge? Tom asked.

The knowledge required goes along with the skills. Our CFO needs to understand GAAP and tax accounting so we prepare our financials by the rules. She also needs to understand how our general ledger and supporting administrative systems work. In addition to accounting, she needs an in-depth understanding of credit agreements and how to apply financial models such as forecasting and net present value, Ryan said.

That sounds like a lot of knowledge. How does Allison's stack up?

Allie came to us from an accounting firm, so she knows GAAP accounting and the systems side well. But she never dealt with a credit agreement or bank before, so this has been a learning experience. The credit agreement has its own accounting rules for what's included in profit. I think this is where Allie may have gone wrong. However, she's intelligent and is picking it up, Ryan said.

Yes, knowledge can be gained. As long as one has the appropriate talents. It sounds like Allison does.

So, we've already touched on Allison's experience. In general, what experiences would be ideal for your CFO to have?

In retrospect, we may have been better off hiring someone with CFO experience versus someone out of an accounting firm. At the time, we were not contemplating taking on debt. Allie was drinking out of a fire hose as we negotiated the credit agreement. All we needed when we hired her was a solid accountant. As I'm expecting to eliminate the debt, I think what we will need most going forward is a strong accountant

OK, what relationships are important to the CFO role?

The key relationship right now is with the creditor. They need to have confidence in our CFO. Other key relationships are with our professional advisors in the accounting and tax area. Allie must have a solid relationship with the partner in our audit firm. She must occasionally deal directly with the IRS and other regulatory-type people. I wouldn't go as far as to say she needs a close relationship with them, but she needs to know how to handle them. Government workers are a different breed.

It sounds like Allison knows how to get along with people, said Tom. I also suspect she can use some of these relationships to shore up her lack of experience in some areas, such as income taxes.

That's true, said Ryan. As long as you know what you don't know!

Great point. Tom lifted his coffee cup to his nose and took in the aroma. He sipped the coffee. What do you think about the French press coffee? he asked Ryan.

It's good. Ryan chuckled. But I'm not going to smell it.

Maybe coffee isn't worth the time to get perfect, but you would agree people are—right?

Of course, Tom. The analogy only goes so far!

So, based on our quick overview of Allison, I would say she is a keeper, Tom said.

I agree, Ryan responded. I think Allie has the talent to learn any skill or knowledge needed to grow further into the role. She's struggling a little bit right now, but as she gains experience, she gets better and better.

It sounds like your number one priority is to do whatever it takes to save her. Any further communications with her? Tom asked.

She sent me a fairly long email apologizing for her overreaction. I think we'll keep her, but no doubt we'll need to make some changes. Like getting her some more competent help to ease the burden.

Now that we've been through the capabilities with Allison, what would you say about Ed?

On the positive side, Ed knows the business and has great relationships with veterinarians. He's skilled at one-on-one selling with traditional owner-operated hospitals. He's an old-school veterinarian that is a naturally good salesperson. This worked well when we were a local operation in the rural Midwest. However, Ed now manages a sales team spreading out across the country. The veterinary profession is undergoing consolidation. This means we are now oftentimes selling into procurement professionals versus veterinarians that own the hospital. He also oversees a digital sales operation that appears to be running without him. Ed just doesn't seem to have the skills or knowledge to do these things competently.

The question becomes does he have the talent to learn these skills through experience or training? Tom asked.

This has been going on for a few years now, so he's gained the experience without gaining the skills. We also sent him to a couple of complex sales seminars. He came back and did nothing different. I'll have to admit we just threw digital sales at him, but we did hire a young guy who has a lot of experience selling B2B online. I don't get this though. Ed's a very smart guy. Learning to sell to large hospitals is not rocket science. If you can become a veterinarian, you'd think you could learn anything.

That's where the broad area of talent comes in.

Our minds are no different than our bodies in that they are naturally good at some things and not others. Remember Michael Jordan in the '90s? He was the world's best basketball player without a doubt but wasn't even a good minor league baseball player. No matter how much he worked, he was never going to make the MLB, let alone be the world's best outfielder.

In Ed's case, he's smart and his brain is wired for science. I'm sure chemistry, biology, and math come easy to him. Also, applying these disciplines to animal health is something he's passionate about.

Dealing one on one with practicing veterinarians is close to home for Ed. It puts him near science and caring for animals. Selling to procurement managers with business degrees is foreign to Ed. He doesn't speak their language or share their interests. It's merely a business transaction to them. To Ed, it's personal. It's about science and taking care of animals. I'm sure he feels empty in dealing with these people, and it shows.

It sounds like you don't think he's going to change, Ryan said.

Never say never, but I think even if he did, it would be like Michael Jordan sticking with baseball. I think you need to have an explicit conversation with Ed and hear what he has to say. I'm sure he's not feeling great about the way things are going and on some level knows he's no longer in the right job. My guess is he's not very happy.

I suppose I've known for a while this has to happen. I've just been focused on all these other things and hoping Ed will turn around on his own.

As the old saying goes, hope is not a strategy! Let's quickly go through your other key people. How's Becky, your HR manager?

Good, said Ryan. This isn't a super complex area with only fifty employees, but you have to get things like payroll and benefits a hundred percent right. Becky is detailed and cares about our employees. She's not perfect, but when she makes a mistake, she owns it and fixes it ASAP. She's reliable. I rarely need to get involved in HR issues other than things like deciding how much to spend on benefits.

From our previous conversation, I assume you are happy with Carol, your Chief Veterinary Officer? Tom asked.

Carol's great, Ryan responded. She understands the science and runs a meticulous lab. It must be that way. If you mix the compounds wrong one time and it kills a dog, your reputation is destroyed. Word travels fast in the veterinary community.

What I also like about Carol is she understands veterinarians. As I mentioned, she helps Erin, our marketing manager, craft messages that resonate with them. I don't like all of our marketing materials—the language for the descriptions and benefits are overly technical—but I'm not a scientist. Even still, I think the language has to make sense to veterinarians even though I find it overly technical. I rely on Carol heavily here.

Nobody's perfect, and one thing I think Carol could do better is being a little tougher on her people. She's kind of a motherly type and protects them. It's not a huge problem, and of course, the staff loves her. I just think it's better if people are given the chance to grow on their own.

I agree that's a potential problem, especially if you continue to grow as you have been. And this could be a talent issue that will be tough for Carol to change. However, I don't think this is an imminent problem. You can put it on the back burner for now—I'd continue to watch it, though.

Speaking of Erin, Tom continued, what's your assessment of her?

Marketing is becoming a big deal for us. Creating a national footprint requires a lot of awareness building. We are, of course, in the veterinary publications; we attend the conventions and do email campaigns. We give Erin a healthy budget to engage an advertising agency that has experience with other businesses in the animal health space.

Erin works well with both Carol and the ad agency. Between the three of them, I think our marketing is effective in getting the word out about National. Erin's a good marketing blocker and tackler. I think she's just what we need at this point.

OK, said Tom. Let's take stock in where we are on people. You have some work to do to help Allison, but she's getting the job done and has the talent to continue to grow into an excellent CFO. Carol is a strong Chief Veterinary Officer that runs a tight ship but may be a bit too gentle with her staff. Becky is doing a solid job with HR. And Erin is what you need right now in a marketing lead role working with Carol and the ad agency.

Ed is one of your partners and responsible for sales. You have serious concerns that as the business has grown, Ed may no longer be the right guy for this role. You need to start having some serious conversations with him. Good summary?

Yes, that puts things into a nice perspective, Ryan responded. I noticed you haven't brought up David, my other partner.

As I recall, you said David was good at his logistics job but oftentimes goes missing. Can you expand on that? Tom asked.

First, I have to say we don't have huge problems in getting our products delivered. Occasionally, we screw something up, but David has the right people and vendors supporting him.

But when we've had some issues lately, they couldn't track down David. For example, we have a huge hospital chain client in Los Angeles who was expecting a shipment on a Monday. It was a rush order that was received Friday morning, and our pharmacists had to work the weekend to complete the order. A lot can go wrong in a situation like this, so David will usually babysit the order from start to finish. This is a big, demanding client that uses its size to get what it wants. On the other hand, they are reasonable in negotiating prices and pay their invoices on time.

When the order came in, the call center immediately called David to take direction. David didn't respond to calls, texts, or emails all morning on that Friday, so they, of course, called me. I ended up essentially doing David's job for him. I shepherded this order through an expedited process so we could satisfy the Monday delivery requirement. I didn't hear from David until the following Tuesday.

When he finally returned my call, he said he went away for the weekend. He turned off all his devices so he could relax and come back refreshed. I told him that although I could understand this, he should have at least let me know. He gave me a half-apology.

Let me ask you. Does David have the skills for his job?

Yes.

It seems like he has the knowledge, experience, and relationships. Is there a lack of some talent? Tom asked.

I don't think so. David studied logistics in college. He was a top performer at Big Pharma. I don't know what's going on with him.

I don't mean to get personal, so don't answer if you're not comfortable. As an owner, has David taken out so much money that he doesn't need to work?

I wish, Ryan responded. I mean, we've paid ourselves some dividends when we had a particularly good year, but most of our cash flow has been invested back into the business. From a compensation perspective, we target paying ourselves market value for our jobs.

So, David needs to work? He doesn't have a lot of money from some other source?

As far as I know, David needs to work.

Let's get back to David later, Tom said. There's still one other person that we have hardly discussed at all. A real important person.

I think we got 'em all, said Ryan.

What about you?

Oh, said Ryan chuckling. I thought CEOs were immune to critical analysis. That we were perfect because of the fact we are the CEO.

I'm glad you're chuckling because that is exactly what many CEOs think. Not just CEOs, a lot of C-level executives believe they are exempt from self-improvement. They believe the fact that they made it to the C level is evidence that they are doing everything right. Things will get better only when other people up their games.

Years ago, when I was an accounting manager for a large insurance company, the CFO was not happy with the timeliness and accuracy of our closing process. He was often embarrassed when after giving the CEO the net income for the month, it would change.

He hired a consulting firm that took us through this improvement process. Of course, I knew the real problem was the CFO would come down to the accounting department in the middle of the closing process and grab a preliminary P&L. These P&Ls were in the process of going through all our checks and balances. However, he would see the preliminary bottom line and let the CEO know what it looked like. This was crazy because the number almost always changed by design. The CEO had no clue what was going on. The CFO gave him a number, so he assumed it was right.

During the improvement process, I asked the CFO what he was going to do differently since we were all being asked to change. He stared at me with a perplexed look and said he didn't need to change. That was the end of that conversation. The consultants eventually took their big check and went away. We got back to business.

Sounds like something that would happen at Big Pharma, Ryan said. I guess all big companies are alike.

I don't think this is just a big company executive phenomenon, said Tom. I believe just about anybody with power starts to believe their own bullshit—pardon the expression. I've known many entrepreneurs that have a hefty amount of arrogance.

Where would arrogance come into the SKERT people model? Ryan asked.

That's a great question. Remember that skills, knowledge, experience, and relationships can all be increased with focused effort. Talent is a broad category that includes intelligence, predispositions, core values, and personality. These attributes can be changed but not by much. They are hardwired into your being.

One could argue that an abundance of confidence is what gets people into positions of power in the first place. We are a society that loves and rewards self-confidence. Arrogance can look like self-confidence, especially when you don't know someone very well.

Also, although I'm not a psychologist, I'd be willing to bet there is a correlation between extreme self-confidence and risk-taking. Entrepreneurs are risk-takers. I think most big company executives took pretty big risks to get separated from the crowd as they moved up the corporate ladder.

So, I think arrogance is part of a person's personality and, therefore, a talent. But people are extremely complex, and various personality traits work together. For example, if an intensely competitive person realized they needed to swallow their pride to win, they would likely do so. It depends on which personality trait is dominant. I'm in way over my head here. I'm just giving you my thoughts based on my experience. Please don't quote me to *Psychology Today* magazine! Tom laughed.

It's like what you were saying yesterday. That our strengths can become our weaknesses.

I think that's right. We already talked about your ability to get things done and how that may be holding back other people and, therefore, the company. What do you say we go through the needed attributes of the CEO for National and see how you stack up?

Do you think I may end up having to fire myself? Ryan half-joked.

Based on what I've heard so far, I doubt it. My guess is we will find some opportunities to improve. However, it is not uncommon for companies in your stage to replace the founding CEO with a CEO having a different profile. I distinguish the two as the founder having an entrepreneurial leadership style versus a professional style.

The professional has experience doing all the things we have been talking about. Getting the right people into the right jobs. Delegating authority. Developing and communicating clear goals and a strategy to achieve them. And putting in place the policies, procedures, and controls to produce predictable results that meet the expectations of your key constituents.

I think you should keep an open mind. If you decide to hand the reins over to a professional CEO, you can still play the role of chair, allowing you to oversee the CEO. You would just need to be extremely careful not to meddle. But we would have to analyze you first to see if that's needed.

You're making me nervous, said Ryan. But let's do it.

Tom and Ryan discussed the capabilities needed for the National CEO to be successful. They differentiated between the capabilities needed in the past versus what will be needed in the future. Ryan supplied most of the past capabilities, and Tom coached him on the future capabilities.

Tom summarized their conversation on a napkin:

	Past	Future
Skills	Sales, Firefighting, Creating new processes, Procuring needed expertise, Running lean	Motivating through purpose and vision, Goal setting and Strategic planning, Hiring and leading effective executives, Delegating authority
Knowledge	How to sell to veterinarians, Veterinary compound pharmacy needs, Basics of pharmaceutical science, Regulations and safety protocols, Delivery costs and options	Principles of effective leadership
Experience	Marketing and selling pharmaceuticals to veterinarians, Putting together a team of people, Delivery and logistics	Formal planning, Delegating authority, Building effective processes
Relationships	Owner/operators of animal hospitals, Veterinary pharmacists, Logistics experts, Compound pharmacy regulation experts, Creditors	Executive coach for CEO, Earned trust of executives and other employees
Talents	High energy and risk appetite, Drive to get things completed, Organized, Motivational thru personality	Patience, Self-awareness, Discipline

Ryan, these future capabilities are pretty much a full-time job. The CEO needs to be spending their time creating the future. To do this, you need to let other people run the day-to-day business. If you have the right people and processes, it should not take much of your time to know things are on track.

I can see it won't be too difficult to acquire many of the skills, knowledge, and experience to be this future CEO. But earned trust? I'm concerned it will be too hard for others to earn my trust to the point that I can let go of the day-to-day stuff.

Tom nodded. You have to be committed. If you think about it, you will still be trusting yourself, but in a different way. You will be trusting the people and processes that you put in place as opposed to your involvement in every decision. So, the question is how much do you trust yourself?

I don't know, Tom, spinning it to mean I am trusting myself may be taking it a bit too far!

Fair enough, but this is why I believe you need a new relationship. An executive coach, or even coaches. Maybe you need a strategy expert to get the planning process going and an HR coach to help you hire and motivate your executive team. This is no different than hiring a banker to help raise capital. These things are no less important to long-term success.

I'll give this some thought, Ryan said. I don't suppose they will be cheap.

It's an investment that should have a tremendous rate of return. If it works, it could prevent you from making a fatal mistake. How much would that be worth? Tom responded.

The to-dos are adding up here, Tom. I need to be sure I can keep Allie on board, have a heart-to-heart conversation with Ed, be watchful of Carol's babying instincts, and oh yeah, change my management style. Is there anything else before we move on with our Saturday?

What are you going to do about David? Tom asked.

Oh shit, Ryan responded. That's a tough one because I have no idea what's going on with him. Maybe he doesn't even know.

Under the talents capability is the broad concept of our personalities. The flip side of how we manage, which we've been discussing about you, is how we want to be managed. Most people that are good at their jobs like to be left alone. Maybe an occasional check-in and "good job," but that's it.

David was doing well at Big Pharma and gave up the big corporate career to join you. Although he is an officer of the company and 12.5 percent owner, I wonder how different this job is for him. How much rope do you give him? Do you think he feels like an executive and owner?

I don't know, said Ryan. Do you think these disappearances when I need him are a little f-you?

Could be. I know you said David needs to work, but I think you risk losing him if you don't act soon.

What do you suggest, another conversation? asked Ryan with a hint of sarcasm.

Of course. A CEO's job is about communicating, communicating, and communicating!

I think you need to sit down with David and get him to talk about how things are going, for example, (a) has National met his expectations, (b) does he enjoy his job, (c) does he feel fairly compensated, and (d) what can you do to further engage him. My guess is he will open up, and you will find there is a lot you can do to increase his engagement.

I suspect David will agree with the CEO behavioral changes we have been discussing. He will likely welcome more autonomy and perhaps take a lead role in things like strategic planning. You'll need the help.

Based on your description of David, it sounds like he could be key to your transition. He has all the skills, knowledge, experience, and relationships the company needs from his position. He also likely has the talents to do more, but they need to be nurtured. I think if you include him in your journey, he will reengage in a big way.

As Tom waived to the server to bring the check, Ryan's phone rang. Ryan got up and walked to a private corner in the coffee shop to take the call.

Ryan returned as Tom was charging the coffees to his room.

Hopefully, that was your wife, said Tom.

No—speak of the devil—it was David. He's fuming mad. One of our salespeople refused to take a return on an order the hospital said we doubled up. It's a big hospital group, and David knows the procurement manager from his Big Pharma days. We're lucky the procurement manager called David, or we may have already lost the account.

Anyway, David called Ed, who was dismissive of the situation. Remember Ed doesn't care for procurement managers? So, David called the sales rep directly. The rep told him he was under great pressure to increase sales, and since the hospital had made a mistake in filling out the paperwork, he felt they should pay for it.

The good news is David is showing some engagement here. The bad news is what is going on in our sales department!

Tom responded, Ryan, I know we've been spending a lot of time together, but this might be a great segue to discuss the second organizational muscle group—community. How do you feel about meeting by the pool at two this afternoon? They will have a trivia game going on, and we can grab a table.

I'm not sure what community has to do with a sales rep acting stupid, but I'll be there, said Ryan as he got up to scamper off to his room. By the way, thanks for the coffee lesson and coffee. And, of course, the great advice. See you at the pool.

Tom called the server over and asked for a paper cup to take the remaining coffee in the French press to go. Once she returned, Tom filled the cup and headed to the pool in search of Susan.

In a Nutshell

- Getting the right people is any leader's first priority.
- Getting the right people requires matching the capabilities needed for excellent job performance with an individual's capabilities.
- Five broad individual capabilities form the acronym SKERT: skills, knowledge, experience, relationships, and talents.
- Current positions should be evaluated using the SKERT capability model, and any gaps need to be filled through education, training, shifting responsibilities, or terminations if necessary.
- The SKERT capability model should be used in making future hiring decisions.

TRIVIA AT THE POOL

Building Community in the Sun

Accept the fact that we have to treat almost anybody as a volunteer.

—Peter Drucker

People were gathering around the far end of the massive star-shaped pool as resort employees were setting up the trivia game. This was a popular activity as the hotel gave away free future stays to the winners. Luckily, a few tables with bright blue umbrellas were still empty to the far left of the stage. Tom rushed to grab one of the tables that would offer protection from both the hot desert sun and most of the noise and commotion. He saw Ryan and waved him over.

A pool server wearing the resort's red uniform was making the rounds and asked Tom if they wanted anything.

As Ryan approached the table, Tom told the server he'd like a virgin piña colada. Want something to drink?

Sure, said Ryan. I'll have an iced tea.

The two men sat across from one another preparing for another probing conversation. The smell of suntan lotion all around them went unnoticed.

I hope you got to spend some time with your family between coffee and now, Tom commented.

My wife was, of course, wondering what we're up to. She at first accused me of doing what we came here to get away from—work! I spent a chunk of this morning sharing our conversation with her. She was intrigued and even got excited. She thinks I should try anything to get out of the work trap I am in. And if by doing so, we can improve the business and not have to worry about money, that would be pretty awesome, in her opinion.

Tom cautioned. Ryan, you need to be careful not to get too far ahead of yourself. We are skimming the surface of the work that needs to be done. I'm sharing concepts that have been written about by hundreds of business professors, consultants, and big-name executives. The reason they keep writing these books is that hardly anyone puts the ideas into action. So, the problems persist, and a new generation of book readers gobbles up the next book only to continue to do things the way they've always done them.

Remember when we talked about executives believing they don't need to change—only everyone else does? The attitude is, "Hey, everyone, here's a book on how John Doe turned around XYZ Corporation. I need you all to read it and do the same thing." It's absurd to think this will work, but I don't think I'm exaggerating.

I get it, Tom. Things are easier said than done.

Yes, but I don't want to discourage you. Just being here now is a great sign you will be willing to do the work. Why don't I summarize where we are at? So far, we have created a "muscular" framework for a healthy company, using the three muscle groups: (1) People, (2) Community, and (3) Process. We called this PCP.

Any organization must get the right People into the right jobs. Human capabilities can generally be described as the combination of (1) Skills, (2) Knowledge, (3) Experience, (4) Relationships, and (5) Talents. We called this SKERT for short. We did a high-level analysis of your key people and you with this capabilities model.

Community is what pulls people together. To get everyone rowing together, a company needs a common purpose, vision, goals, and strategic plan.

The last muscle is Process. These are the detailed policies, procedures, and practices that tell people what to do and to keep things under control. Remember, the definition of control is achieving predictable results based on an objective. A company is a conglomeration of various processes, each of which has its objectives that fit into the whole.

Our conversation this morning ended with you getting a call from David describing a sales rep's treatment of a big customer. Any issue should be looked at from the prism of the three muscles. Is this sales rep in the wrong job? Or is he a good guy that doesn't understand National's purpose and vision, and values? Or is the company lacking specific policies, procedures, or practices that would lead to the desired behaviors consistently?

We, of course, don't have enough information to analyze this sales rep, but do you know much about him?

Yeah, I know him fairly well. He's been with us for a couple of years and has a reputation for hitting his numbers. He's been around the veterinary pharmaceuticals business for over a decade.

Why do you suppose he took such an inflexible stand with a key customer? Tom asked.

Our sales have not kept up with our expenses, and we have been putting a lot of pressure on the sales team. We found there was a misalignment in how we paid commissions. The commission rate being paid was too high for serving existing customers and too low for signing up new accounts. This encouraged the sales reps to focus on existing business at the expense of growing new customers. To solve this, we adjusted the sales pay plan so they could make as much money overall, but they had to do more cold calling to get there. Some reps have not stepped up and have seen their compensation go down. I suspect this rep may be in that category.

Tom leaned back. That may explain it, but it doesn't answer the question about which muscle group the problem lies in. Is this a character flaw, a misalignment of values, or a bad policy? By not viewing the problem through the three-muscle prism, it is difficult to determine. Since we can't psychoanalyze this poor rep this afternoon, let's talk about the second muscle group, Community.

Community is made up of Purpose, Values, and Strategy, or PVS. I apologize for continuing the use of all these acronyms, but I find them helpful to remember. As you will likely be talking about these things, you'll need to find your way to communicate the concepts effectively.

Purpose answers the basic question of why your business even exists. We talked about this a little bit at the bar last night. We all must do something to make a living. Most of us choose a job, trade, or profession to serve various existing organizations. We do our own personal SKERT analysis and try to maximize our compensation for the capabilities we possess.

To get the most out of us, organizations need to offer more than a paycheck. People are more engaged if they believe in the purpose of the organization they serve. We are also more engaged when we share values with the organization and know where it is headed.

Companies that engage employees rather than merely employ them enjoy a competitive advantage. Almost any product, service, or process can be copied in today's world. People move around and so much information is so easily available. However, you can't copy a company's high-employee engagement. People are too complex, and engagement is unique to each organization. But I believe it starts with having a noble purpose that people believe is filling a need in the world.

Capitalism gets a bad rap because of the inequality of it. It certainly does create inequality, but it is also perhaps the most equalizing institution in history. What some people don't understand is the value of risk-taking. Society only improves when people with new ideas take out a second mortgage to start a business. Very few people have the risk appetite to start a business. Therefore, we must reward these people who happen to succeed, or we won't have any new businesses.

Most employees are happy for their owners to get rich if they believe in the purpose of the business. In some cases, I've seen employees take pride in making their owners richer. On the other hand, I've seen businesses where the owners are greedy, and the employees are resentful and disengaged. Which businesses do you think perform better?

I've got to believe the business where employees are happy to make the owners richer.

Indeed. So, the first step to creating a community of engaged employees is to create a shared purpose, Tom continued. What would you say is the purpose of National?

I started this business to help veterinarians get compound pharmaceuticals from an animal health company at a reasonable price versus having to go to local human pharmacies that were gouging them. Pet owners that have small or large pets should not have to pay an arm and a leg for the same medicines average-sized animals get inexpensively. Much of our business is making medications easier for animals to take as well. For example, if they don't like the taste of a medication, we can make it taste better or maybe convert it from a solid to liquid, whatever it takes to get the sick puppy to take his medicine. You know, like Mary Poppins.

Is your customer the veterinarian or animal owner?

Both, said Ryan. Our primary customer is the veterinarian. We take orders from hospitals, and they pay us directly. However, we sometimes deliver the medicines directly to the animal owner. If the animal owner is not happy, it gets back to us, so we have to treat them like a customer even though we go through the veterinary hospital.

It sounds like your purpose may be simply ensuring that all animals have access to the medications they need to stay healthy, Tom said. I'm sure a marketing type could make this sound more inspiring, but that is a meaningful purpose if you love animals.

I like it, said Ryan. I think we could use something like this to get our people focused on the value we provide. We're saving animals' lives!

Think of all the stories you could tell around this purpose. Animal lovers will work for free! Tom said, jokingly.

Ryan put up his hand and stopped the conversation. Hold on, Tom. They are doing American history trivia. I've got to do this.

The hotel trivia moderator asked over the speaker, What year was the American constitution written?

Oh, that's easy, said Ryan. Seventeen eighty-seven.

The moderator confirmed the correct answer was 1787.

Well, I knew it was about then, said Tom.

The Constitution is an amazing document, Ryan said. It was radical at the time and provided the framework and rights that have created this great country we live in.

This is a good segue into **Values**, the next component of creating a community, said Tom.

Although the United States has people with a wide range of values, most people agree on some basic values—such as those spelled out in our founding documents. Any organization needs to have shared values to hold it together and guide its people. You may not need a constitution, but you need something.

Ryan, you are the founding father of National. Just like the founding founders of the United States put effort into instilling common values in the people of the newly formed country, you must instill values into National. If this is not done consciously, it will happen implicitly. The question is—do you know what these values are so people can share them? I don't mean to bring politics into the discussion, but I think Facebook might be a good example of having clear company values. Mark Zuckerberg states publicly that he and his company value all viewpoints. However, conservatives, including powerful senators, accused Facebook of favoring liberal points of view. You can disagree with these conservatives, but just the fact that they can make the point suggests that Facebook has not been clear on either (1) deciding its core values or (2) communicating them to employees. Instilling common values in any company is difficult as each employee brings their own values to work. However, if you want your employees to live by certain values, you must be explicit about it and work at it constantly.

Hopefully, this example can help you see where not having clearly defined, shared values can lead your company into doing things that go against its interests. Have you given values much thought?

Not in an organized manner, Ryan answered. I usually talk about values when something goes wrong. For example, when we get a customer complaint where we didn't do the right thing, I will talk about how we value our customers.

Valuing customers is good, but it's not a core value. A core value is a person's principles or standards of behavior, one's judgment of what is important in life. An example of a core value might be integrity. Integrity is the quality of having strong ethical or moral principles and always following them, no matter who's watching. A person with integrity acts with honesty, honor, and truthfulness.

Got it, said Ryan. Integrity should be a core value of every organization.

I told you about a pet health insurance company I worked with years ago. I like that example because you are in the same general animal health space. The company had four shared values: Passion. Integrity. Respect. Courage.

Passion was focused on the mission of the business. Employees were passionate about helping pets get optimal medical care by taking affordability out of the decision process.

Integrity was about meeting commitments. The company believed that meeting commitments was the highest form of integrity.

Respect is the grease that allowed people to work effectively together over time. The company had titles and formal authority, but all people were respected as individuals. The attitude was that although not all jobs were compensated the same, all jobs were critical to the success of the company.

Courage was mostly about doing the right thing even when it was politically dangerous. The CEO liked to tell the story about a project he was passionate about. It was a big project involving every aspect of the business. Although the weekly reports said things were on track, he was apprehensive. Something didn't smell right, but the whole team pushed back when he expressed concerns. One day he was chatting with a frontline customer care employee who told him he needed to kill the project. She gave her reasons, and it confirmed his fears. Based on this courageous and unsolicited feedback, the CEO was able to get the team to admit it was off track and agree to terminate the project. Millions of dollars and months of time were saved.

Let's see how these four core values interact with valuing the customer. If employees are passionate about the business, meet their commitments, and are otherwise honest, treat all people with respect, and act with the courage to do the right things, do you think they will take care of your customers? I think so.

However, you will find many companies state that they explicitly value their customers. I don't see a problem with this. After all, ultimately the customer pays the employees' salaries. But people forget this and pay attention to what their boss wants because the boss determines their pay and can fire them. Customers don't have this direct power over employees, but it would improve service greatly if they did! Companies that make customer service a core value are trying to mimic this.

On the other hand, I think this can sow confusion. You mentioned that you had two customers, veterinary hospitals and animal owners. Many companies have what could be considered multiple customers. Any business that distributes its products through other businesses has this issue, for example, a manufacturer that sells through retail stores, an insurance company that sells through independent agencies, or a cruise line that sells through travel agencies. The intermediary and the ultimate customer are not always aligned in terms of what they need or want. So, who do you value more? By sticking with core values instead of stating you value customers generally, you avoid this type of confusion and get people focused on virtuous behaviors that can be applied to all constituents.

Other common values I've seen in corporate value statements include diversity, innovation, learning, and leadership. What do you value, Ryan? Because as the founder and CEO of National, the company's values must be consistent with what you value. You will need to walk your talk, and this will be impossible if you don't believe in the values you put forth.

Ryan pondered for a few moments. I've never given this deep thought. I believe in outstanding customer service and, of course, integrity. However, as I sit here, I think one of our core values must be science. Veterinarians and animal owners are administering our products into animals with the assumption our medications are properly compounded and will work. And certainly not hurt the animal.

Tom suggested, Maybe this could be described more generically as trustworthiness?

I like that, said Ryan. Trustworthiness extends to animal owners, veterinarians, employees, and even capital providers such as shareholders and creditors.

I've also always liked the "golden rule" of treating people the way we want to be treated. This would be like the "respect" value your pet insurance company had.

Another thing is speed or a sense of urgency. Our world is moving faster and faster, and people's expectations of getting what they want when they want it is forever increasing. Whether delivering products to customers or providing a coworker a piece of information to complete their job, we need to move fast. But also be accurate.

To summarize, I'd say the values that resonate with me are (1) the golden rule—treat people the way we want to be treated, (2) be trustworthy by doing the right things the right way, and (3) have a sense of urgency in getting things done.

I think that's a great start, said Tom. Keep in mind you can't come up with purpose and values statements in a quick conversation. They must be true to you, but you also need to get input from your executive team. Ultimately, you need buy-in from all your employees. This takes a series of meetings and communications over time.

Once you codify your company purpose and values, you need to talk about them as much as possible. Share stories that demonstrate people living the purpose and values. They need to be constantly reinforced so they become clearer over time and a cultural norm. Also, new employees need to be formally educated. Although once they are ingrained in your culture, newcomers will be indoctrinated through observed behavior.

This is the first time you mentioned the word culture, Ryan said. Is that really what you mean when you talk about community?

That's a really good question, Ryan. I think culture is the amalgamation of the company's purpose, values, strategies, policies, processes, and daily interactions of people. In other words, culture sits beside all three muscle groups. It's not a muscle as much as an outcome of the muscles working together. Maybe call it the soul of the organization.

Every organization has a culture, whether intentional or not, for better or worse. You can usually describe a culture in a word or short phrase. For example, a sales culture or a culture of fear. Once a culture is in place, it is difficult to change. You can do it by explicitly working the three muscle groups. Getting the right people, creating a community, and developing effective processes. This is not an easy task, and it typically takes up to two years to complete.

The pet health insurance company I keep coming back to had a culture of fear and entitlement when a new CEO took over the company. It was losing money and people were fearful it was going to fail. Also, the previous CEO had both a tyrant and a soft side to him. He yelled and screamed at people while at the same time not holding them accountable. This created additional fear but also feelings of entitlement.

This deeply rooted culture prevented the company from breaking out of its downward cycle. The new CEO quickly identified that the key to fixing the company was changing its culture. To accomplish this, he worked on strengthening all three muscle groups to transform the company into a culture of confidence and accountability. It took about eighteen months, and it worked!

So, when you are engaging in a process to change the results of your company, there is a good chance this includes changing the culture. A healthy culture is indicative that all the muscles are in good shape so results should be good. It's, of course, no guarantee. For example, not all business models are winners. If customers don't want to buy your products at the price it takes for you to earn a fair profit, the results are not going to be good—no matter how awesome your culture is.

Hang on, said Ryan. I'm hearing an animal-related trivia question.

The game host then asked over the loudspeaker: "How many years ago were pigs first domesticated?" Ryan guessed three thousand and was surprised the answer was nine thousand.

Ryan said, When I was at Big Pharma, we sold a lot of antibiotics to pig farmers to cure swine dysentery. My compound pharmacy business is 100 percent geared toward companion animals so we don't get those huge orders for herds. I wish!

The next question was "What do you call a group of toads?" Ryan correctly answered a "knot" as he was allowing himself to be pulled into the game.

Tom stepped in and suggested this question was a good segue back to culture. Ryan apologized for getting distracted.

How would you describe the culture of your National "knot," Ryan?

We're not a bunch of toads, Tom, but sometimes, it may feel like that. I'm probably the wrong person to answer your question. When I think of our dominant behavior, I think we are all practicing crisis management. Everything becomes a crisis, and we have become actually pretty good at this.

I've known some people that like working in a crisis environment, and they will create one when one doesn't exist, said Tom. However, I think this leads to stress and burnout in most people. And stress leads to mistakes.

We have our share of those, and this could be why people are so willing to have me bail them out. They are just tired of the stress.

That's insightful, Ryan. You may be right. So, your question about culture was a great one. Part of your communication process will be the shift in culture required to improve National's results. You will, of course, need to gather some data and confirm that people agree with your assessment of the current crisis culture.

I'm pretty confident they'll agree! Ryan said with a smile.

So, what should the culture be?

What would be great is a culture of decisiveness. I'd like people to make decisions and implement them. Of course, I want them to be sound decisions. But I believe we could move so much faster if we were more decisive in both deciding and then acting on it.

This is going to be even more important as we go forward. We are seeing competitors pop up, and the human pharmacies are not happy about losing their veterinary hospital business. Especially the big chains. National needs to get nimbler.

That makes sense, said Tom. I've got to believe the lack of effective decision-making is creating the crises. So, a big goal of strengthening the National muscles will be moving from a crisis culture to one of decisiveness.

Again, I must warn you, Ryan, that all this needs to be carefully orchestrated with your management team. I would not barge into your next management meeting and declare you are changing the culture from crisis to decisive. This all should come out of conversations you can lead, but you need to let them come to their own conclusions. You may be surprised. Good and bad.

Would you suggest we use a facilitator?

In my opinion, it's best to self-facilitate these kinds of discussions. However, not every CEO has these skills. Self-facilitation can lead to biased results or swirling. At a minimum, you need a skilled scribe to document the key elements of the conversations. The scribe can also act as a timekeeper.

It's also important that you properly prepare for the meeting. This is where a facilitator adds perhaps the most value. We are getting ahead of ourselves, though. We have a lot more to discuss. We haven't touched upon strategy or process yet. I think once we get through all the muscle groups, we can put an action plan together. Assuming we don't run out of time! Let's move on.

I appreciate your help, Tom. You're doing a great job helping clarify what I need to do.

Thanks, Ryan. Helping executives like you is one of my passions. I believe well-run businesses are the most important contributor to a healthy society. Think what the world would be like if everyone were happy working at good-paying jobs for companies whose purpose they believe in? I think we'd all be getting along much better!

You're a dreamer, Tom, but that's OK. One company at a time.

Tom smiled. Yes, I am. All right, so far we talked about getting the right people and creating a community through common purpose and values. This led to a discussion about culture. Culture is an outcome of exercising, or not exercising, all three muscle groups. But culture is something that should be explicitly considered when driving for business results.

The third aspect of building community is strategy. It is the S in PVS. Purpose. Values. Strategy. Like all this stuff, a strategy is easier said than done. It starts with a goal that needs to be specific and time-based. Strategic goals are big and generic. They could be as bold as becoming the market leader in your business by a certain date. Or maybe doubling your sales in three years. You must be able to measure your goal or it won't be helpful.

Setting goals that everyone agrees to is not always easy. This is because people need to believe they are attainable, and you will likely have differences of opinion on this. Or you may get disagreement on the importance of conflicting goals. A typical tradeoff is revenue versus profits. You can grow revenues, for example, by reducing prices. This, of course, reduces the gross margin and likely profit. Marketing and salespeople will usually fight for increasing revenues while finance watches out for profit.

A good debate is healthy, but an agreement is critical to gain the buy-in required to "row together" in achieving the goal. A strategic goal must be supported by a strategic plan. Due to the broadness of strategic goals, all areas of the business must contribute. This requires each area to create subgoals that support the strategic goal.

The pet health insurance company I keep bringing up struggled for years to stay in business. They were constantly raising equity to pay the bills. At the time, pet insurance was a new market and pet owners were unsure of its legitimacy. Therefore, the company could not get the prices it needed to earn a profit. The company needed a new strategy.

By paying attention to his customers, the founder realized they were interested in wellness care. Consequently, he broke the insurance norms and offered an insurance wellness rider that covered certain wellness procedures such as annual visits and shots. The business exploded.

This required every function in the business to create new objectives. For example, sales and marketing had to create a different approach to gaining new business. Claims had to develop a process for handling wellness claims. Underwriting and finance had to figure out how to price the wellness product and any impact it would have on existing product profitability.

Unfortunately, this is where the company lost control. They started to grow rapidly without thinking through the ramifications of this strategy being successful.

The strategic planning process is, therefore, an exercise in (1) establishing a goal, (2) evaluating the capabilities required to achieve the goal, (3) assessing your current capabilities, (4) measuring the gap between the required and current state capabilities, and (5) creating a plan to fill the gap. The pet insurance company jumped into a new strategy without doing any of these and got itself into trouble despite increasing sales.

Creating a plan to fill the gap can be painful. First, no company has unlimited resources. You can't do everything you ideally need to do when you need to do it. The plan will force you to match available resources to what's needed to achieve the goal. You may conclude you need to either adjust the goal or figure out how to get more resources, for example, raising equity or debt.

Even after matching resources to action steps, a company will find it can't do everything at once. It must carefully prioritize and have contingency plans if things go wrong. In my experience, setting priorities is another area rife with conflict. Each discipline tends to think it is the most critical to the business and will fight for as many resources as it can get. This is where the CEO will likely be the good guy and bad guy, depending on what they decide.

The CEO must do what they believe is best for the business. Setting priorities should not be a function of "taking turns." I once worked with the CEO of a specialty auto insurance company. This was during the recession of 2009, and the company was struggling for revenue. The claims department had been screaming for a new system for years and justified the cost/benefit for a new system. The CEO made the firm decision that until the company started getting sufficient revenue growth, all discretionary spending would be funneled to sales and marketing. This sent a clear message on what was important, and everyone understood, even if they may not have liked it.

I think one of the most common mistakes CEOs make is having too many priorities or allowing priorities to shift as the environment changes. I met a CEO once who had just completed an annual offsite strategic planning process. He was beaming that they had sixteen clearly defined initiatives. They were all sure to move the needle forward.

I knew he was in trouble. Having too many priorities is like having no priorities. And sixteen was way too many.

Let me ask you, what do you think happens when you have too many priorities?

You don't get any of them done? Ryan answered tentatively.

That's right. There are just not enough resources to do them all. Furthermore, it creates an environment where A for accountability is replaced with A for effort. It's obvious everyone is working hard—despite nothing getting done. However, once accountability is gone, the game playing can begin—in other words, telling yourselves that everything is all right because you are working so hard.

A powerful way to think about sticking with priorities is to consider the value of a project. You decide to do a project because it is going to increase revenue, decrease costs, or improve the business in some other way that will presumably increase its value.

So, what adds more value to a business: having one project 100 percent completed or any number of projects partially completed? No value is created until something gets done!

This ties in well with a culture of decisiveness, Ryan said, making decisions and seeing them through to the end. I think you've hit on something, Tom. In our crisis management mode, we oftentimes shift priorities and never get back to many things that seemed important at the time. I can only imagine the wasted time and resources spent on things that never finished and therefore never added value.

Exactly. This is why strategic planning is an ongoing discipline and not an annual one-time event. As difficult as it is to come up with goals and a gap analysis, once this is done, the hard work is just beginning. Once everyone goes back to their desks after the strategy meeting, they are confronted with the real world. It's messy. We become distracted by what appears to be urgent issues. The strategic initiatives get put on the back burner. Before you know it, a year has gone by and issues that were critical to achieving the strategic goal are incomplete.

So, what happens then? asked Ryan.

You're not in control. Remember we talked about control being the predictability of outcomes. When a management team allows events and circumstances to dictate its priorities, predictability becomes impossible. We can't predict what tomorrow will bring. You may still meet your goals, but you may not. It depends on how the gods of fortune treat you.

To be honest, many companies don't have strategic discipline, and they do all right. It depends on their business model. A business model is a trendy term for describing what value a company provides its customers. It is products targeted at a certain customer at a price point that generates a level of profitability after paying all expenses.

I worked with a company that enjoyed a great business model. They had products they could manufacture and distribute at costs far lower than what their customers were willing to pay in price. This profitability made up for a lot of sloppiness. They did not plan at all. However, they never lost sight of their customer and they understood the competition. Although they were profitable, I believe they underachieved and ended up selling the company for less than it was intrinsically worth.

I suspect there are not many companies in that situation, Ryan said. Most markets are so competitive that prices are pushed right up against expenses. Market leaders find ways of keeping prices down without giving up profits so competitors must scramble to catch up.

We're finding that in our business. At first, we had a lot of room in our prices as we were competing with local human pharmacies that had no competition for the veterinary business. These pharmacies saw us come into the marketplace and quickly take a good slice of their profitable business away from them. They began dropping their prices to veterinary hospitals and even started to market to them. We woke them up!

And now we have other companies popping up that are veterinary specific, just like us. Their prices are tough to beat. Either they know something we don't know, or they are trying to buy market share.

Great point, Ryan. Competitive analysis is a big part of strategic planning. You must know what your competitors are doing to ensure you remain competitive! Back to the pet health insurance company.

They had a full-time professional staff person that did nothing but track what the competition was doing. Any changes in products, prices, advertising, websites, etc., were tracked and documented. The marketing team used the information to craft messages to combat any smart advertising being used against the company. The department created a laminated information summary for the sales staff showing the best way to sell against any of the company's twelve competitors.

This information was summarized for use at the annual strategic planning meeting. For example, the company was finding small competitors could look big online. In a strategy meeting, management decided to use its superior financial resources to hire the top digital ad agency in the country to "win on the web." This strategy worked as the online closes skyrocketed.

The company could have been distracted by many things, but it stayed focused on the digital sales improvement process. The CEO had a saying that the top priority should get "fed first." In other words, people should work on the top priority with any discretionary time before anything else.

Strategic planning should, therefore, create some pressure on the executive team. This shouldn't be a comfortable process. Tension is created by the gap between the goal state and the current state. Management should feel a sense of urgency in filling that gap. And this tension usually gets more intense as the year progresses and project milestones become due.

There should only be a few strategic initiatives each year. Each initiative should be assigned an executive owner who is primarily responsible for its achievement. A project plan, including key milestones, must be developed with the management team receiving a full status report at least monthly. Without this discipline, any initiative has a high likelihood of failure.

I'm starting to see how I'm misallocating my time, Tom. I'm not doing any of this stuff. I haven't put forth any specific goals. I have an intuitive sense of our current capabilities but don't spend any time organizing it into an improvement plan. We don't have any formal strategic planning sessions other than an annual budget meeting. The business is running me—I'm not running it!

That's pretty common with smaller or early-stage companies. You don't need to have this formalized structure because the CEO can keep it all in their head. However, once you get to a certain size, you become spread too thin. Too much time goes by between interactions with key people. Without a plan, they spend time on what they think is important, which may or may not align with what the business needs.

We have pretty much described where you should be spending your time between this morning's discussion about people and this afternoon's discussion about purpose, values, and strategy. If you're not spending a vast amount of your time on these issues, you are right in saying the business is running you.

This is another good segue into the last of the three muscle groups: process. A good process is what allows you to spend time on these higher-level issues. The keyword is good. Ineffective processes will eat up all your time. They are, therefore, strategic imperatives. You can forget about any initiative to move the business forward if your core processes are deficient. They will derail you.

The trivia game was winding down. At the beginning, about two dozen people were playing sitting around six tables. Half the players had left as the sun was hot and their chances for winning eliminated. Empty glasses, bottles, and nacho plates were scattered across the deserted tables. It was down to two people as to who would win the free weekend at the resort. One was a professorial-looking gentleman who looked to be in his sixties. The other, a young woman with several friends who were clearly having a good time and helping her out. Their table was covered with empty beer bottles.

Ryan and Tom listened in on what was to be the final question: "Who sang a duet with Ed Sheeran on the song 'Perfect?'"

Tom laughed. I'm about that guy's age, and this question is loaded with age discrimination. I've heard of Ed Sheeran and that's about it.

The professor answered first and was clearly guessing when he said "Madonna."

The young woman and her entourage began jumping up and down in jubilation as she screamed out the correct answer. "Beyonce!"

Tom turned from watching the trivia game to face Ryan. Ryan, we have talked about so much. I think we should spend a few hours with our families and get back together at the fire pit tonight. The process muscle will require some time to go through. Its importance is often underestimated, and I want to make sure you have the full picture.

I appreciate your spending so much time with me. This is good stuff—although I can see it's not easy stuff. If you are willing to give me the time, I'll be super attentive tonight. Would nine o'clock work?

It does for me, said Tom. See you then.

In a Nutshell

- After getting the right people, a leader needs to build a community that includes PVS: Purpose, Values, and Strategy.
- Employees will be far more engaged in the success of the business if they understand its purpose and how it contributes to society. Leaders need to be clear on the business purpose and communicate it to employees at every chance. A good starting point is to craft a purpose and vision statement.
- Values drive behavior and play a key role in how a company is perceived by all key constituents. A leader needs to be in touch with their own values and be explicit on what the company values are. Creating a common set of values provides needed boundaries for employees as they deal with one another, customers, and other people outside the company. A good starting point is working with a cross section of employees to write a company values statement.

- People need to know where they are going, how they are going to get there, and how they are doing. This is accomplished with a strategic plan that sets goals, provides an honest assessment of the current state, describes the action steps to get to the desired future state, and lays out the specific initiatives each function must achieve within a given time frame. A good starting point is having a facilitated strategic planning meeting with the senior executives.

THE FIRE PIT

Predictability and the Smell of Quality Cigars

Making good decisions is a crucial skill at every level.

—Peter Drucker

The property had numerous fire pits scattered about. The largest was adjacent to the main bar off the lobby; it was a round structure of brown and ash sandstone about three feet high and ten feet across. The stone was capped with a smooth light-gray concrete rim. In the cool evening, the gas fire pit was a welcome sight, with its large black tumbled lava stones. About a dozen large rattan chairs with red cushions surrounded the pit, each with its own side table.

Ryan approached the pit looking for two open chairs next to one another. As he moved toward a couple of chairs near the pit, he heard Tom shout out from the bar area: Ryan, over here.

Ryan walked over to Tom, smiling. Hello again!

Tom had a couple of cigars in his hand and waved them so Ryan could see them. Do you smoke at all? he asked.

I do enjoy a cigar once in a while.

I picked up cigars late in life, said Tom. I like to have one or two a week. If it were up to my wife, Susan, it would be zero. She really hates them!

My wife is actually OK with cigars although I don't smoke very often.

Unfortunately, said Tom, we can't smoke at the main fire pit. However, there is another one down the walk that is for smokers. Let's grab a drink and walk down there.

I'm buying, Ryan insisted. What would you like?

OK, since we now know each other better, I'm going to order my own concoction. It's a spin off the Rob Roy. A blended Scotch whisky with two maraschino cherries and a splash of cherry juice. The cherry juice is lighter than sweet vermouth, and the scotch taste is more prevalent. Just sweetened up a bit.

Ryan ordered Tom's drink and a neat Jack Daniels for himself. They got their drinks and headed to the smokers' fire pit.

There was no one there when the men approached. They took adjacent chairs and positioned themselves for ease of conversation. After placing his drink on the table nearest to his chair, Tom took the cigars out of his pocket. The plastic covers crinkled as he unwrapped both cigars and handed one to Ryan. I hope you like these. I've tried various brands, and a friend suggested these Rocky Patel LB1s. I love them, but I know people have different tastes.

Tom pulled a combined cigar lighter and cutter from his other pocket. Here, Ryan, you can use this to cut and light it.

In a few minutes, the cigars were lit. The aroma of high-quality cigar smoke filled the air.

Tom settled further into his chair. I just can't understand why my wife hates the smell of cigars. To me, the aroma is part of what makes the experience relaxing.

Cheryl likes the smell. She might have joined us if she knew! Ryan chuckled.

What makes a good cigar, Ryan?

I don't know . . . mild taste and smooth burn?

Taste is personal, but we would all agree on a smooth burn. The reason I like Rocky Patel is their consistency. I can rely on getting the same flavor in every cigar. Also, the Patels are always easy to light, burn evenly, and rarely go out. I get an easy draw that makes every pull effortless and relaxing. And I don't suppose it's luck.

I feel a segue coming, said Ryan.

Remember how we discussed that just like the body needs to exercise all its muscle groups, a company needs to exercise its three muscle groups. We have already discussed the first two—people and community—so tonight, we will talk about process. And, yes, I do think cigar making could be a good analogy to start with. First, let's assume we are only talking about hand-rolled cigars. Hand-rolled cigars are made up of 100 percent tobacco, which gives them a better scent and flavor than machine-rolled cigars.

Given the way handmade cigars are constructed, it allows for the creation of endless flavors and consistencies depending on where the tobacco is grown. However, the entire process requires hundreds of people. From planting tobacco seeds to transplanting small plants to the fields, fermenting, destemming, and ultimately rolling, many people are involved. It is a series of processes that must be under control. In other words, they must have predictable outcomes.

Cigar smokers count on that predictability. If they are disappointed even once, it could lead to a lost customer. My guess is these cigar makers are careful to hire the right people that happen to love cigars, spend tons of time training them, and create a great community so that turnover is low. Also, they likely have numerous controls or checkpoints to ensure the series of processes are achieving their objectives. Given the physical nature of the product, I assume there would be physical tests of some sort. These are the processes we need to discuss next.

Ah. I see. In theory, cigar making is not much different from our veterinary compound pharmacy. We also make a consumable physical product that must be mixed with 100 percent predictability. Predictability is even more important for us as a bad mix could harm or even kill an animal. Once that gets around, we would be at risk of losing a lot more than one customer. We could lose our reputation.

Yes, but before you can build sustainable business processes, you need to establish a control framework. In my experience, there are four essential elements to having a strong control framework:

- a commitment to integrity and ethical values,
- a clear Delegation of Authority,
- an established Policy on Policies that sets up all the individual written policies and procedures the company requires,
- a system that holds people accountable to the agreed-upon objectives.

We discussed values and culture around the pool earlier today, including things like integrity and respect. However, behaving with integrity and ethical values is not optional, no matter what your company's core values are. These values are foundational to the fidelity of the organization.

For example, what would you do with a top performer who lacked integrity and one day stole money from the company? It doesn't matter how much money; this would not only be a lack of honesty and integrity, but also illegal.

I'm not sure, Tom. If it were a top salesperson who controlled valuable contacts, I'd be torn. If we let them go, they could compete against us and take clients.

Yes, but what are the long-term consequences of looking the other way? First, you send a message to the company that integrity is not important. If someone is stealing money from you, that person lacks integrity. People may not know that person stole money, but they know the person lacks integrity from their interactions. So, they won't likely be surprised to learn the person stole money.

So, a small theft may turn into a big theft. Or this lack of integrity manifests in some other form such as cheating clients. Or other people see what's going on and think it's OK, so they join in. With time, the market sees that you are not a company that can be trusted and stops doing business with you. This is particularly true in your business where you previously told me trustworthiness was critical to your success.

Ryan nodded in understanding. Short-term pain for long-term gain?

Yes, people are complex. Even if they behave ethically today, it does not guarantee they will tomorrow. Things happen in their lives that may move the ethical bar. Unimaginable behavior today can be rationalized tomorrow by a change in life's circumstances, such as divorce, a disabled child, or caring for aging parents. A company must have empathy for people but also be clear about its ethical standards. For example, stealing from the company will result in termination and prosecution, period. This "red line" will save some people from themselves.

I get it. But what do you do?

You need to codify your behavioral expectations in a Code of Conduct. A typical Code of Conduct requires employees (1) abide by the law and any relevant regulations, (2) maintain a healthy and safe environment, (3) avoid conflicts of interest, (4) protect proprietary and confidential information, and (5) respect the property rights of others. The code is also where the purpose and values of the company are documented.

Each new employee should be provided a copy of the code and sign off that they have read and understand it. Any substantiated violation of the code must lead to disciplinary action up to and including termination.

This code sets the tone of the organization. That it will be law-abiding and behave with integrity and ethical values. This tone will be felt by all constituents such as employees, customers, vendors, regulators, shareholders, and the community. You are setting the tone for being a trustworthy entity. At a minimum, this should afford you the benefit of the doubt should something go wrong.

I can't stress enough that the code is a worthless document if not enforced. Management must take the appropriate disciplinary action when an employee violates the code. No matter how valuable they are to the organization. And the behaviors of the CEO and executive team must exemplify the code. Leading by example here is essential.

I'm not sure where I'd begin writing a Code of Conduct.

Like I said, you can't do everything we're talking about alone, and you can't do it all at once. Some things can be done simultaneously, and you will need to prioritize, of course. And you will need to spend some money on help. I suggest we get through the process muscle and then come up with an action plan.

OK. That would be great.

The second item you need to create a control framework is a formal Delegation of Authority. Delegating authority means—delegating authority. You are allowing, really expecting, other people to make certain decisions. Of course, responsibility comes with authority. An employee is expected to accomplish something with this authority and must be held accountable for those responsibilities.

One warning here. Remember that there is a big difference between delegation and abdication. You can give up authority by delegating, but you remain responsible. Walking away from responsibility entirely after delegating authority is an abdication and is dangerous.

On the other hand, people need a little room to fail. There is no better learning experience than failure. This is particularly true with less-experienced managers and employees. We just want to make sure we don't fail too big or too often. People will appreciate sufficient oversight to ensure they meet their responsibilities.

Tom tapped his cigar on the edge of the fire pit. Delegation of authority is something that happens throughout the organization. Much of it is informal. For example, a manager needs a project completed and delegates it to one of their reports. Hopefully, the scope and objectives are clear, and a protocol exists to track progress. The delegated authority should be discussed upfront. It becomes the employee's responsibility to get it done. However, the manager is still responsible in your eyes. So, they have an interest in ensuring the employee succeeds.

I've too often seen managers assign work to employees and then walk away. When things go wrong, they, of course, throw the employee under the bus. Sometimes even firing them as a scapegoat to save their own status. If this happens enough, people will feel unsafe and stop making even small decisions, creating bottlenecks up and down the chain of command. Results will suffer.

I've gotten a little ahead of myself, Ryan. Let me get back to the control framework. The formal Delegation of Authority is a written document that lays out what positions have what level of authority. The authority is typically described in financial terms. As the majority owner of the company, you may delegate yourself an unlimited authority. However, this may not be wise since the minority shareholders would likely want a say in matters that may significantly affect the value of their stock, for example, taking on debt for an expansion.

There are two types of activities regarding formal authority. The authority to spend money now and in the future. Spending money now simply requires the approval of an invoice. Spending money in the future is more complicated. It requires deciding who has what authority to enter contracts. And to further the complication, contracts are sometimes vague in terms of what future remuneration will be required.

Also, some relationships have consequences beyond financial, for example, potential conflicts of interest and competitive sensitivities.

A formal Delegation of Authority spells this out. I assume you don't have any document formally delegating authority to you or your staff?

That's right. Although we keep things informal, Ed and David pretty much go along with what I think we should do. Occasionally, we disagree but have never had a strong disagreement that caused significant issues between us. They were nervous about taking on debt but eventually saw that it was a risk worth taking. Debt would allow us to grow the value of their stock.

Although a formal delegation of authority is not as critical in a relatively small company like National, it becomes more important as the company gets larger. For example, if you sell equity and take on more shareholders, they will likely want board representation. These new shareholders won't have the close history you, Ed, and David share. Therefore, they will want more structure around who has authority for what. In other words, the board will be delegating authority to the CEO, leaving key strategic decisions for themselves. If this delegation is not clear, I can assure you that problems will occur.

For example, I was involved with a company that had a long-standing, independent Board of Directors. The CFO left the company, and the CEO hired a new one without involving the board. While nothing in writing indicated that the board needed to approve the hiring of a CFO, it had been customary to do so, given the importance of this position and its relationship to the board. The board was so agitated with this situation, it fired the CEO. This may have been the straw that broke the camel's back, but had the board approval of the CFO position been a formal policy, this may have been avoided.

The CEO is typically provided broad authority as they have complete responsibility for running the company. The CEO can, of course, delegate authority to their direct reports. For example, the CFO may have the authority to sign checks up to a certain amount. The marketing executive may have the authority to enter into contracts with ad agencies up to a certain dollar amount with maybe a few agencies prohibited for competitive considerations. And so on.

Furthermore, your executives and their direct reports can delegate their authorities. For example, if the CFO can sign checks up to $100,000, they might allow the controller to sign checks no greater than $10,000. The purpose of delegation is twofold: (1) It provides the delegator the time to do their most important tasks, and (2) provides the delegatee the opportunity to feel they make a meaningful contribution while learning. This helps ensure you are getting the best out of the great people you hired and took all that effort to align via Purpose-Values-Strategy.

Again, this is right in line with my wanting National to be a decisive company. If we have people down the organization that can make sound decisions, we can push more and more decisions down, allowing us to move faster and faster without losing control! This would create a virtuous cycle as our employee turnover would be lower, and the people we have get better and better from their positive learning experiences.

That's right, Ryan, and it starts with a formal Delegation of Authority. Even if at first it is rather simplistic. Having one makes you conscious of the need, and it can evolve with the company.

I know you want to discuss action steps after Process, but can I ask who would be responsible for writing and maintaining this Delegation of Authority? Ryan asked.

You and the executive management team would have to own it. In other words, approve the original document and any changes. However, you can assign one of your executives to be its author. I typically see this being either the CFO or head of human resources. Oftentimes they work together.

Makes sense, said Ryan. Thanks.

OK, let's move on. The next document you need to build your control framework is a Policy on Policies. This policy establishes processes and standards for developing, reviewing, approving, amending, and decommissioning specific company policies. It also lists the core policies that the company will have. These can change, of course, but you need a starting point.

Company policies are important as they set expectations for employees in all the areas we have discussed, including performance, values, and behavior. They also enable accountability, help ensure compliance with applicable laws and regulations, facilitate treating employees fairly, and help defend against various types of legal claims.

Typical policies a company should require include:

- Employee Code of Conduct
- Delegation of Authority
- Human resources
- Equal opportunity
- Substance abuse
- Workplace and cybersecurity
- Compensation
- Travel and entertainment
- Social media and email
- Attendance, vacation, and time off
- Workplace health and safety

Oftentimes policies are only considered after something has gone wrong. For example, perhaps an employee uses social media improperly, giving the appearance they are speaking on behalf of the company. This could not only damage the company's reputation but also put it at legal risk. A social media policy explains what is and is not acceptable for employees online when representing the company. A policy that has been shared with employees is strong evidence that any misuse of social media would be due to a rogue employee. This protects the company legally but not likely its reputation. Therefore, it is critical that policies be effectively communicated and available for employees to read at all times. Their purpose is to encourage the right behavior and prevent things from going wrong.

Writing policies and procedures is hard work. Maybe this is why so many companies don't do a very good job of it. And once a policy is written, it is even more difficult to ensure it stays current and relevant. The first step is to identify the need for a policy. Some are standard, such as travel and entertainment, since this has been a part of business forever. On the other hand, a social media policy was not needed in most companies even ten years ago.

Once you identify the need for a policy, you need to determine the content. A human resource policy would include hiring, training and development, and termination practices. As HR is so broad, there are typically other stand-alone policies that could be considered part of HR. What to consolidate and break out separately is a judgment call to be made by the company. However, things like compensation, workplace safety, and paid time off are usually significant enough to warrant their own document.

Ryan broke in. Tom, this is really in the weeds. Is this something the CEO needs to be spending time on?

I know, Ryan. This is the point where the CEO's eyes glaze over. You shouldn't be writing the policies, but you can't abdicate responsibility for them either. You have to be involved and make sure you know what's in them. There are going to be decisions in each of them you will want to weigh in on.

Let's take HR practices, for example. Do you prefer promoting from within or hiring fully trained people from outside the company? Is low employee turnover an objective to achieving your goals, or do you just need bodies? Are you willing to pay for recruiters that can be very expensive or have your internal HR staff recruit? These questions and others need to be answered before you can write an HR policy. I believe the CEO should be part of the conversation. Once you have all the questions asked and answered, the HR executive can craft the policy for sharing.

Every policy needs to go through this same drill. By explicitly considering and documenting the various policies, you can summarize, crystalize, and distill how you want things to work. Once completed, the policies need to be shared and communicated with all who are expected to follow them.

The pet health insurance company I've mentioned a few times had grown from a start-up to nearly $100 million in revenue. Recall it changed its strategy, which created rapid and substantial growth. However, in addition to not having a strategic plan, the founder and CEO never put in place formal policies and procedures. Therefore, nobody knew what to expect, as decisions were arbitrary and inconsistent.

When the company was small, the founder could be involved in nearly every decision. To the extent he was consistent, there was some predictability. But as the business rapidly grew to hundreds of people after they started selling the insurance wellness rider, managers had to make decisions. And as you might imagine, without guidance, they were all over the place.

Each manager applied their personal judgments and values in making decisions. This created inconsistency. When employees can't predict how management is going to react, they will close down. Information that should be shared is withheld—especially if that information is bad news. Therefore, problems are hidden until they explode. This is one of the causes of crisis management that we previously discussed.

Documented policies and procedures are not bulletproof. Most people don't sit down and study them. Their value is in the upfront thought that must go into them. It forces you to think about how you want certain things to be operationalized. For example, travel and entertainment policies will ultimately be reduced to a form people must fill out and a process of checks and balances to make sure the expenses are appropriate. It will need to include what expenses are reimbursable, documentation required, approval process, etc.

Even though people may not study the policies to ensure they are following them, it is critical to have written policies to support disciplinary action when they are violated. A violation could be a one-time event based on an employee not being familiar with a policy. This requires educating the employee. A documented "policy and procedure" is needed to do this effectively. Repeated or blatant disregard for following policies and procedures requires more serious discipline up to and including termination.

Ensuring policies and procedures are followed allows for control of the organization. They are the rules of the road. Even outstanding people that are aligned to your company purpose, values, and strategy need to know the specific rules of engagement. Think about the chaos that would ensue if everyone just did what they thought was best.

One impact would be people unknowingly violating an applicable law or regulation. This is particularly dangerous in the area of human resources. There are so many regulations designed to protect employees from disparate treatment. If managers are not trained to follow these rules, they are likely to make a mistake. This could lead to employee lawsuits.

Let's say a manager makes a comment trying to be funny but that is offensive to a legally protected group. Now assume an individual in the protected group finding the manager's comment offensive works in their department. The person heard the comment first or secondhand. And let's say this employee is underperforming and was about to be disciplined for shoddy work. This whole process is now compromised. Is the manager biased and singling out this employee or holding them to a higher standard? What was a straightforward performance discussion may now be more about the company's behavior toward this protected group. Depending on the personality of the employee, this could become a legal action against the company.

Now you may say you know the manager is not biased; they were just trying to be funny. And that the employee has been underperforming for a while and is using this comment to save their job, etc. The fact is the employee has a point. The manager made a comment which brings their objectivity into question.

How do you prevent such an unfortunate situation? Having good HR policies and procedures that are effectively communicated is the way. In this example, you'd still have the problem if the manager made the comment. However, if it did devolve into a lawsuit, the company would argue that the manager violated company policy and its liability is therefore limited. There are several protected groups with which this could happen. Keep in mind gender is no longer a simple matter. The binary categories of yesterday are melting away to the true complexity of human beings. The world is moving so fast, it is hard to keep up. But companies must keep up and have current policies that reflect today's realities.

Is this making sense, Ryan?

Yes. I think what you are saying is as long as a company is small, you can almost single-handedly control everything. You are close enough to all the employees that you are the control point. However, as you get bigger, you lose this ability and become dependent on managers to make day-to-day decisions and people behaving in a manner consistent with expectations. The company must essentially codify behavioral expectations so that its employees know what is expected.

This would be pretty powerful in my situation. In effect, it would give me the ability to sleep at night. I could rely on the policies and procedures to do this part of my job for me. This would both increase the probability that they would do the right thing and save me time.

Tom interjected. Not just the time required to get involved in the primary decision but also time spent cleaning up messes. Also, one person could never have all the knowledge required to keep the company safe and on course. You would always be subject to not knowing what you don't know.

OK, said Ryan, but how do you know how you are doing? You can't afford to wait to see if you accomplished the goal when the buzzer goes off, right? That would be too late.

This time you have provided the segue, Ryan. The fourth step of building a control framework is creating accountability. Remember we talked about delegating authority. People cannot be responsible without having authority. If I make you responsible for something, it isn't realistic for me to expect you to complete it without giving you the proper authority and resources. If I keep all the authority, I keep all the responsibility.

Although a manager can delegate authority, they cannot give up responsibility. If you delegate responsibility and the delegate fails, you share in that failure. So, you want to ensure your delegation is successful. This is where accountability comes in.

As CEO, you delegate authority for nearly every major function of the company. The CFO runs the details of finance. You are not approving journal entries or signing checks. The same for HR and down the line. If any of these functions break down, you are ultimately responsible. In your case, it just means as the majority shareholder, you suffer the financial impact. Most CEOs are employees and subject to Board of Director oversight. Material breakdowns in any major area of the company can cost a CEO their job.

Many executives convince themselves they hold people accountable because they are quick to reprimand, but lecturing or scolding people is not holding them accountable. Accountability requires consequences. Employees in many ways are no different than children. You have children, right?

Yes, I have an eight-year-old son.

Tell me, does it work when you tell your son over and over again not to something? Does it work when you yell at him and then go back to doing what you were doing?

Of course not, Ryan answered.

Right, we all know this to be true. Yet we continue to expect it to work with both our kids and employees!

Thousands of books have been written on leadership, and effective leadership is critical to success. The books are usually written by a celebrity CEO who thinks their leadership style can and should be emulated. They typically team up with an educator that helps put the leadership style into some sort of organized framework. All of these books have something to offer, and many are worth reading. But just reading a book is not likely to change behavior.

The leader sets the tone through their behavior. CEOs in particular have enormous power within an organization. It is difficult to get the truth when you are the CEO. People simply behave differently when you are in the room. They are on their best behavior with you. Many will agree with you and tell you how smart you are even as they're thinking you're ignorant and wrong.

I'm telling you, as CEO, you should not even trust your best friend. People know one mistake interacting with the CEO can be career-limiting—or ending. Thus, they behave accordingly. Once in a while, you may find the rare individual who tells you what they really believe. These people are a gift, although many leaders see them as not being on board and discard them to their detriment.

I'm sorry to interrupt, Tom, but leadership seems so important I'm surprised it's not a separate muscle group.

Leadership is sort of like culture. If PCP is the muscles, leadership is the mind, and culture the soul. The mind has to direct the exercise of the muscles. That's leadership. The culture is what the organization is at its core. A summation of its leadership, people, purpose, and so on. Culture boils it all down to its essence. For example, you want National to be a decisive culture, then creating this culture starts with your leadership. You must not only be decisive yourself but also instill decisiveness in all the muscle groups. For example, look for decisive attributes when hiring people. This would be a talent that can be explicitly built into your hiring practices. Decisiveness can be rewarded in your HR and compensation policies, etc.

The entire control model we are discussing is a form of leadership. I call it "Letting Go Leadership," because it requires you to let go of making every decision and depend on other people and processes to be the control mechanism.

It's a good point, but maybe the mind is not a perfect analogy.

It's good enough for me. Thanks.

At its core, leading people is not really any more or less complicated than raising kids. You need to be clear about expectations, walk your talk, and provide consequences both positive and negative. It's providing true consequences.

I think all parents would agree it's easier to yell at your kids to stop doing something than to take privileges away. When my kids were young, time-outs were in fashion. If our daughter or son misbehaved, they would be forced to sit by themselves and write positive affirmations such as "I respect my mother." The written statement would typically correspond to correcting the behavior in question. This may sound simple, but it was a struggle and took patience and discipline on the part of my wife and I, especially with my son who would often just refuse to go along. The hard part was escalating the punishment without escalating the emotions. My wife was much better at this than me. I tended to either get angry and start yelling or give up. Not the best leadership!

In leading people and raising children, negative emotions, like anger, are typically not helpful. These emotions take the focus off the issue at hand and become the issue themselves. You can end up apologizing to the original offender. You lose credibility as the leader. This is why a system of accountability is so important.

You mean like time-outs?

Yes, the adult version of time-outs. We talked about a control framework that includes a:

- Code of Conduct
- Formal Delegation of Authority
- Policy on Policies
- System of accountability

Time-outs are a system of accountability for children. Whether they are not eating their carrots or displaying disrespectful behavior, time-outs are the consequences intended to discourage such behavior in the future, creating a culture of tranquility.

OK, what does the adult version of time-outs look like?

First, I need to provide some perspective. We've been talking about the process muscle that works with the people and community muscles to keep an organization in control. Specifically, we've been talking about the components of a control framework up to this point. The process muscle also includes the detailed "policies and procedures" listed in the Policy on Policies and process documentation, which is somewhat different. For example, everyone fills out the same travel and expense report and is expected to follow the company's social media policy. We typically expect full compliance with policies and procedures, and any deviation is considered a failure needing corrective action. Processes and process documentation are different.

A process starts with inputs and includes a series of steps taken to produce the desired outcome. In your business, for example, you take pharmaceuticals as input and remix them for a specific purpose. This includes remixing doses for breed size, changing the flavor to make it more palatable, or converting a pill to syrup for easier consumption by the animal. Although many of your products are popular enough to predict need, you also frequently receive unique orders to fill promptly.

Another business process would be sales. The inputs into this process would be product, price, promotion, and placement. The sales activities include online sales as well as sales generated from the sales team interacting with the customer. The outcome is revenue and unit sales resulting in a gross margin.

As I mentioned before, any company is a conglomeration of its processes. And these processes often impact one another. For example, information from the marketing process feeds into the sales process. If marketing gets it wrong, the sales process will have little chance of success. Therefore, a good marketing department would be wise to use the sales process as a critical input.

It is helpful if each process is documented. Just like with policies and procedures, this forces you to summarize, distill, and crystalize what you want out of the process and how it should work. Processes typically evolve with the business and are sometimes created on an ad hoc basis. This can result in the processes being sub-optimized. Businesses are constantly changing, and processes need to adapt. This will happen implicitly, but it is far better to be thoughtful about it.

Here's an example from my experience as a customer recently. I have lousy teeth; I'm always going to the dentist. I had a great dentist. However, she sold her practice and moved out of California. A dental consolidator bought the practice. I assumed this would be a good thing, maybe provide more services so I did not have to go to a separate specialist for things like a root canal.

The new owners replaced my dentist with a young dentist seemingly right out of dental school. I didn't like the new dentist for several reasons. One day I was in for a cleaning, and a different dentist saw me. I liked him and asked if I could switch. They told me he was just filling in that day and was from a different office. It turns out the office he worked out of was closer to my home. Perfect! Well, not quite. Since I was a patient of this particular office, I had to use one of its dentists.

I'm sure there are all kinds of internal reasons for this process. And that it resulted from trying to consolidate not just this office, but many acquired practices. However, the new owners, not dentists, by the way, assumed that a dentist was a commodity. Well, as I'm sure they'll learn the hard way, a dentist is not a commodity. They have a special relationship with their patients based on trust. I found another dentist, and I suspect many other patients have as well.

Processes are impacted by systems. I worked with a company once that had one hundred customer care professionals taking calls. These employees handled everything from simple procedural questions to serious complaints. At the time, the company had no customer care software to manage the process. If you know anything about call centers, this is unimaginable. Employees literally had to raise their hands to ask permission to go to the restroom!

As you might have predicted, the turnover in the department was through the roof. Nearly seventy-five percent. This compounded the problem, as the time spent training people was enormous. It wasn't unusual for customers to wait thirty minutes to get a rep on the line. And then the reps were both inexperienced and in bad moods because they'd been getting yelled at all day by understandably angry customers. Although a new system would cost about twenty thousand dollars to start, buying the system was a no-brainer and should have been done long before. The cost of lost customers and employee turnover dwarfed this investment.

This was an example of the CEO not understanding that the company had changed. In the beginning, the calls were so few that no system was needed. Also, twenty thousand dollars was still considered a significant investment. However, having a hundred reps means you have the revenue to invest, and you better do it!

Putting in a new system forces you to document the process. Again, documenting processes is a great way to ensure you are optimizing them. Not all process inefficiencies are as obvious as the two examples I just gave. Oftentimes, when you document a process, you find simple steps that can be eliminated or made more efficient. Such as uploading an Excel file to an accounting system versus manual reentry.

Although optimizing processes is important to keeping costs down, the most important aspect is ensuring each process objective is achieved. For example, if I were running the dental consolidator, I would have an objective of minimizing patient turnover. Buying a practice and replacing previous owners with employee dentists is going to have an impact on your patients. Losing a bunch of customers up front does not make for a good return on investment.

The company that installed the call center software was able to put in place the industry-standard objective of answering eighty percent of calls within twenty seconds. Within about a year, they were achieving this objective. They also set an even more difficult objective of resolving any customer issue on a single call. This is likely an impossible objective to meet, but just pushing for it drives higher customer satisfaction.

Remember we talked about control. A company is a conglomeration of its processes. Control is only meaningful when attached to an objective. Therefore, each process needs to be assigned one or more objectives. If enough of these objectives are being achieved, the organization is very likely "under control." Meaning it is achieving predictable results. Hopefully, these predicted results are in line with investor expectations.

Ryan mused out loud. A prescription for sleeping at night.

Yes, said Tom, but it's not as easy as popping a pill. Being explicit about process effectiveness and clear on process objectives takes hard work, time, and cooperation. What I've seen the most effective CEOs do is require every executive to set process objectives and update them at least annually. The objectives need to be measurable, so you know whether or not you are on track. Typically, the CFO is responsible for tracking the metrics and accumulating them in a periodic report.

This report becomes the "bible." Each week, month, and quarter, the management team pours over the metrics, comparing each to its objective, the prior period, and trend. The results are analyzed and any corrective action committed to and followed up. In essence, this is the adult version of time-outs. Let's take National as an example. What would you say are your major processes, Ryan?

Let me think for a moment. Certainly marketing, sales, inventory management, manufacturing and packaging, customer service, procurement, accounts payable, accounts receivable, cash receipts, and distribution.

Would you include HR processes such as hiring, training and development, terminations, payroll, benefits, etc.?

Of course. I guess I think of employees as the people doing the processes and not a process themselves. I can see where this might lead to confusion.

Tom continued. People are not a process, per se, but the processes that impact employees are critical. I've always had an objective of zero errors on the payroll. People don't like it when we get their paycheck wrong and will quickly lose confidence in the organization when we do. What objectives might you have for some of the processes you listed?

For sales, we need to hit unit and dollar sales for both our sales team and online sales. Also, we need to maintain a gross margin that drives bottom-line profitability.

Our most important metric for marketing is the effectiveness of our online advertising. This can be measured in website visits, engagement, and conversions. We can probably do a better job at this.

Distribution is all about having delivery times that meet customer expectations. This is where David is really good.

Procurement and inventory management go hand in hand. We need to have the materials to mix our standard products to meet customer needs. For special compounds, we need the ability to source materials in real-time. Just because it's a special mix doesn't mean the sick dog can wait. Also, as these pharmaceuticals are expensive, we have to be concerned about leakage.

Even though you sell something, it doesn't count until you get the cash. Accounts receivable aging is, therefore, something to watch as well. We've had times when our old receivables were way too high. Not only is this bad for cash flow but it also increases the risk of write-offs.

You have a good feel for the metrics that drive your business. What would you say about metrics for employees?

The thing I want most is low turnover. It's so disruptive to the business to lose a good employee. It would also be nice to have some sort of "happiness" metric. In other words, a measurement to gauge how people are feeling about their jobs and the company.

Tom nodded. I agree with the employee turnover metric. It's an indication of the overall health of the company. The happiness metric would be more valuable as it is a more proactive measure. There are survey tools you can use to measure employee happiness or engagement, but they must be used carefully.

So, this brings us back to leadership and the issue of holding people accountable. You can do this at periodic meetings. At these meetings, have your employees go through the metrics that support the achievement of process objectives. These serve two purposes. One, they create peer pressure. Nobody wants to go in front of their peers having not achieved their commitment to the team. And two, if an executive consistently misses their objectives, after ample coaching, a change must be made. Again, the adult version of time-out. This is the only fair thing to do, and the team will support it because the need is clear. It also sends a strong message to everybody that performance is the driver of decisions around people—not politics such as favorites. The company becomes a meritocracy.

Holding people accountable to the achievement of specific objectives has the added benefit of creating a line of sight between the employees and the company's broader goals. This ties into creating a community. The more employees can see how what they do contributes to the overall company goals, the more engaged they will be. It can be difficult to be engaged when you don't really understand why you are doing something or if you make a difference.

This is easier said than done. In my career, I had to fire people I liked because they didn't perform. However, I always gave them plenty of coaching, explaining to them where they were falling short and what the company needed from them. In every case but one, by the time I let them go, they told me I had been fair, and they took responsibility. Other people notice this and feel safe that decisions about people are based on agreed-upon performance. It also encourages them to perform, as the flip side of discipline is financial and promotional rewards for those who excel.

As the CEO, you cast a large shadow. If you hold the executive team accountable and reward them for performance, they will do the same with their direct reports.

We've been at this for a while, and it's getting late. My cigar is long out!

We've covered a lot of ground. Probably a good place to stop and get some sleep. Tomorrow is our last day here, but I think we can pull this all together.

Why don't we get together right around checkout time? If it's OK, I'll ask my wife to join us. Feel free to invite your wife and son. Susan has been wondering what we have been talking about all weekend, so we can show her she hasn't missed anything!

OK, said Ryan. I'll invite Cheryl and Chad, but I'll be surprised if they come. How about meeting in the main lobby at eleven?

Sounds good. I'll have to give some thought to how to summarize all of this, and we can come up with an action plan you can use to take National to the next level!

I'm excited. I believe you have given me a pathway to success, and I'm looking forward to one last meeting!

Tom grabbed both empty glasses and walked them to the round tray used for collecting dishes for washing. Ryan thanked him and headed in the opposite direction toward his room. Tom briskly walked back through the lobby toward his room.

In a Nutshell

- The third and final muscle group for achieving results is process. Good process is required so people know what to do and are accountable for achieving agreed-upon objectives.

- A leader needs to put in place a control framework that includes a (a) Code of Conduct, (b) formal Delegation of Authority, (c) Policy on Policies, and (d) system of accountability. Creating these requires thought, effort, communication, and time. However, they don't need to be perfect at first. The sooner you get started, the more impact they will have.

- Specific policies that establish expected behaviors in certain circumstances should be documented and effectively communicated. For example, travel and entertainment and Human Resources.

- Leadership is the "mind" that directs the three muscle groups. The most important aspect of leadership is holding people accountable to agreed-upon objectives. Actions and results must have consequences both positive and negative. Holding people

accountable to commitments creates an environment where results drive behavior.

- Any organization is an amalgamation of numerous processes. These processes work together to achieve an overall result.
However, each process must have its own objectives that can be
measured and achieved. A leader must ensure processes are effective, efficient, and kept current as the business and environment change. This is best accomplished by maintaining current
documentation of each process and being deliberate about expectations. Process documentation is tedious work that people
generally shy away from. However, the key is to get started with
agreed-upon objectives.

THE WALK

The best way to predict the future is to create it.

—Peter Drucker

The next morning, Tom and Susan went for an early walk around the resort.

Susan said, You've been pretty busy this weekend spending time with your new friend. Don't you ever get tired of talking about business?

I'm sorry, Susan. I hope you had a good weekend despite my absences. You seemed to keep busy, though.

It was fine. Just good to get away from the routine for a couple of days and not have to do dishes and clean and all that stuff. But answer my question: Will you ever tire of talking about business? You've probably given this guy ten thousand dollars of free consulting this weekend!

It's worth it. When someone like Ryan comes along and is willing to listen to my ideas, I can't help but give them to him. I understand that he would be paying a fair amount for this advice from a consultant, but he would likely not do that. And his business would just plod along while his and his workers' happiness decreased. We have too many businesses plodding along out there. We need them to be firing on all cylinders.

You can't save the world, Tom, and you're probably not as smart as you think.

Smart is not an attribute I've ever ascribed to myself. I hope I've made it clear I have never had an original idea. I'm a practitioner, not a theorist. I do think I've learned a lot in forty years of business and know what works. And I'm happy to share these learnings with others, understanding what worked for me may not work for them. But I do think the principles I'm discussing with Ryan are universal. Each individual may have their version, but I'm convinced they work.

I know you've had some success. I've been with you for thirty-five of those forty years. I just feel the need to keep you in line! Susan joked.

You know, I've never taken you through my entire model for what I call controlling a business. Why don't you join us for our last session at eleven today? Just after we check out. You can meet Ryan and his wife and son who may also be there.

I don't know, Tom. I've already gotten a good night's sleep. Just kidding! I'd like that.

CHECKOUT

The Work Has Just Begun

Plans are only good intentions unless they immediately degenerate into hard work.

—Peter Drucker

Ryan, Cheryl, and Chad were all sitting together in the lobby in big soft chairs positioned around a large coffee table. On the table was a square copper vase holding a single white orchid. Ryan and Cheryl were talking while Chad played a video game on his phone.

Tom and Susan approached the sitting area. Tom called out, Hello, Ryan. Good morning!

Ryan and Cheryl quickly rose to greet Tom and Susan. After shaking hands, Ryan told Chad to get up and properly introduce himself. Chad smiled in embarrassment as he pulled away from his game and shook Tom and Susan's hands.

Ryan said, We grabbed these chairs because there are five of them around the table. They're pretty comfortable and I think conducive to conversation.

Great, thanks.

I've been telling Cheryl about our talks this weekend and how I think the ideas are going to help improve our business.

Cheryl said, I especially like the part where Ryan doesn't have to be on call 24/7 and constantly put out fires!

That's up to Ryan, Tom said. Some people just like putting out fires. It's part of their personality, and they will always seek the flames. I do think the fact that Ryan has been such an attentive listener this weekend means there's a good chance he's ready to give up firefighting.

Ryan and I have been through what I call a model to "control" a business or organization. We wanted to get together one more time to summarize the model and come up with a high-level action plan Ryan can take back with him. Cheryl, we thought it would be a good idea for you to hear this too so you can be a sounding board going forward. Chad, feel free to listen in between games. Susan agreed to listen in as she has never had the chance to hear a holistic description of my model. I'm just going to jump in and start rambling. Please stop me at any time with any questions or comments.

Through studying and trial and error, I developed an approach to leadership that got results in three different situations. All three circumstances required a turnaround. The organizations were underperforming and a different approach was needed. I applied these same principles in all three cases, and they worked!

So, this model I'm about to describe is based on experience. I'm not a business school professor that has analyzed dozens of companies and interviewed their CEOs. My experience is with smaller organizations. Entrepreneurial companies start small, and the lucky ones grow. Early-stage companies strive for revenue. They're trying to figure out if there is a market for their products. Most of these companies fail. Some go on to become very successful.

However, success is not simply achieved by growing revenue. At some point, that revenue must produce a profit. As Ryan and I discussed, earning a profit is not the goal of a business but a responsibility. You need to make a profit to earn the right to stay in business.

Long-term success requires a transition. Many small companies do OK until they hit a certain size. They look successful, but then things start to unravel. Revenues are fine but profits don't follow. Expenses start to grow faster than revenue.

I believe this is because the informal control procedures that work for a small company no longer work when a company gets to a certain size. Typically, the founder has tight control over everything when the company is small. This is doable when you have a dozen employees. However, as the company grows, it adds employees. At some point, the founder's control of making all the decisions becomes a limiting factor to growth. Also, they become a bottleneck driving down productivity and the relationship between revenue and expenses. This makes profits elusive.

My model essentially replaces the founder's control over everything with a framework of formal controls they can rely on. That's why I refer to it as "Letting Go Leadership."

Tom, I notice you used the word *control* and then *controls*. Is there a difference? Cheryl asked.

Great question, Cheryl. Control is a verb where one is trying to direct or influence people's behavior or course of action. Controls is a noun and is the specific activities put in place to accomplish control. Control presumes you are trying to achieve a specific objective, for example, a business leader is trying to direct his employees' behavior so the business achieves financial success. How they do this is critical. When companies are small, the founders can achieve control through personal involvement in every key decision. When a company grows to a certain point, it becomes impossible for the founder to maintain control through this force of personality. With so many employees, the founder must rely on managers to make decisions they used to make. It is often hard to let go of these decisions. This isn't just true for entrepreneurs. Many corporate executives, and even managers, suffer from being control freaks—they can't let go and trust other people. Thus again, my model is about Letting Go Leadership.

Controls are the structures, systems, policies, and procedures put in place to ensure decisions align to achieving the company's objectives. In effect, they do the work the founder or executive once did themselves. It is these activities that Ryan and I have been discussing all weekend.

This is not rocket science, and there is nothing original in my control model other than maybe the way I've organized the principles.

However, implementing the model is perhaps just as difficult as rocket science. It requires patience and faith in people and processes, which are not typical attributes of entrepreneurs and executives.

Cheryl broke in. I'd have to agree with you relative to Ryan. Especially the lack of patience.

Hey, this isn't a beat on Ryan session. After a minute, where Cheryl gave him the look, Ryan chuckled. OK. OK. You're right.

That's right, Cheryl, Tom said, and it is this lack of patience that helped Ryan build National to where it is. People, in general, don't like change, and changing personal habits is very, very difficult. I think the more success someone has, the more difficult it is for them to change. After all, they have all this success. Why do *they* need to change?

Keep in mind the importance of the objective. If a company is generating enough profit to allow an entrepreneur to achieve the lifestyle they desire, no change may be needed. We call this a lifestyle business. Many small businesses stay small because it is currently satisfying the lifestyle of the owner. Neighborhood family restaurants and specialty retail shops typically fall into this category. They are local, part of the community, and have carved out a safe niche for themselves.

On the other hand, many companies need to grow. National is a good example. Ryan came up with a new business model that filled a need in the veterinarian profession. Successfully filling this need locally is going to attract competition. In order to survive, a company is going to have to build scale and pursue a national strategy—which Ryan did right from the start. If he stayed local, another company could come in and gain size, eventually taking away his business through the efficiency of scale.

It is likely the compound pharmacy business will gain new competitors and eventually consolidate. Ryan is in a race. If other companies come in and grow faster, this will impede his ability to grow. And as I've said, at some point a larger company will come into his market and either take away clients or offer to acquire National depending on their strategy.

So, Ryan doesn't have the choice of being a small local niche business for long. His products and services are too well suited to being delivered cheaper and better by large companies with scale. Given this situation, he must grow both the top and bottom lines.

If Ryan decides that he wants to grow the business and be a national player, he will need greater profits to invest back into the company to support that growth. On the other hand, if he decides to cede the national platform to another company by selling to them, National's valuation will depend on its historic profitability. In other words, you won't get much for your business if it's not making money. The worst outcome is National fails to grow profitably and competitors put it out of business.

The market is Darwinian. The strong survive. Strength is measured by sustainable profitability. Sustainable profits are food that keeps the organization healthy. And healthy companies keep communities healthy by providing jobs, taxes, and support for charitable causes. Ryan is playing a game of chess with his competitors that impacts far more people than himself.

I hope my husband is good at chess. I feel like Chad and I are two people that will be highly impacted by his game, Cheryl said.

Tom said, In my opinion, Ryan has done a great job getting National to this point, and all options remain open. The company is experiencing some growing pains, and he will need to change his approach quickly to match his chess opponents, so to speak. This is where the control model we've been discussing comes in.

Normally, Susan did not pay deep attention when Tom talked shop. However, she was struck by Cheryl's level of interest and questions. I never thought about business like that before. Obviously, companies come and go and people are impacted. But I never thought about the principal role of the CEO and how one person could be so responsible for that coming and going.

Ryan jumped in. You don't think about it so seriously on a day-to-day basis. On one level, you know you have this responsibility, but you get buried in the flurry of activity.

Tom added, And if you don't act with intention, these activities will drive you instead of you driving the business.

This statement seemed to get Chad's attention. He briefly looked up at Tom. After thinking for a few seconds, he put his head back down to continue his video game.

Ryan and I loosely used a person as an analogy in talking about this control model. The corpus includes three core "muscle groups" that work together in moving the business forward. Leadership is the mind that directs the muscles, and culture is the organization's soul or essence of being.

Leadership style is unique to the leader. Every human being is unique and approaches things differently. This is because individuals will have different visions, goals, and biases. This doesn't invalidate using a model to control the business. It also should give leaders comfort that using a model is not going to replace the unique stamp they put on the business. The model makes them better leaders as the organization becomes more predictable and safer for employees.

Before we get into the model, let me talk briefly about culture. Culture is the behaviors and procedural norms that can be observed within a company—which includes its policies, procedures, ethics, values, employee behaviors, and attitudes. It makes up the personality of a company (e.g., professional, casual, fast-paced). Company cultures are heavily influenced by the people that started them. Their personalities become the personalities of the company. This, of course, can be good or bad.

The control model allows a CEO, or leader, to be more deliberate about instilling a positive culture in their company. For example, Ryan told me he would like National's culture to be "decisive." The culture lacks decisiveness not because Ryan is not himself decisive but because Ryan has not effectively delegated authority. Therefore, managers now needing to make decisions don't know how and hesitate. Although cultures are difficult to change, this is something that can be changed through the control model. I apologize for the long setup.

Tom reached into his weathered black leather backpack and pulled out a yellow legal pad of paper and shiny black pen. He got up and scooted his chair to position himself so Ryan, Cheryl, and Susan could see the pad.

He then drew the following diagram on the pad:

Leadership			
	People	Community	Process
	Skills	Purpose	Control Framework
	Knowledge	Values	Code of Conduct
	Experience	Strategy	Delegation of Authority
Culture	Relationships	Goals	Policy on Policies
	Talent	Future State Needed	Accountability
		Current State	Policies and Procedures (including processes)
		Gap to Fill	
		Priorities	

Pointing to the *Leadership* and *Culture* boxes, Tom said, We've already discussed leadership and culture. Leadership is the mind or brain behind the organization. The leader sets the tone and direction. Culture is the company's soul or essence. We often boil a personality down to a word. "She's cerebral" or "he's outgoing." The same can be done with companies. For example, Amazon "moves fast."

The question is how a leader goes about shaping the culture and driving performance. Do they do it consciously or by happenstance?

Because successful organizations need predictable results that meet the expectations of their key constituents—shareholders, employees, and customers—leading without a deliberate theory or model is risky. I just don't think most companies can do this over the long term without being deliberate.

The control model is such a theory. It guides the leader to do the things required to chart a course and stay on it. As I mentioned before, the control model is the corpus of the corporate being. There are three core muscle groups.

Tom pointed to the boxes on the pad labeled *People, Community,* and *Process.* These three muscle groups work together, just like the muscles in our bodies that are interconnected. For example, you may have back pain that is being caused by a strained buttocks muscle. Just like a healthy body needs all muscles to be exercised, a company needs all three of these muscle groups to be worked. A weakness in one area can cause a failure of the whole.

Ryan interjected, looking at Cheryl. For example, you can hire all the right people, but if you don't build a community or provide effective processes, the model will break down and results suffer.

That makes sense, Cheryl responded.

Tom continued, I agree, but at the same time, hiring the right people is perhaps the most leveraging muscle. For example, let's say you are a high school basketball player and want to jump higher. Although you need strong muscles throughout your body to be good at basketball, your quads and hamstrings are your primary thrusters. In business, people are your primary thrusters.

People are also the most complex and hardest to get right. Think of an individual's capabilities as a combination of skills, knowledge, experience, relationships, and talent. SKERT for short.

Tom pointed at the related boxes on the schematic. Skills are the expertise needed to do a task. For example, a nurse needs to have the skills of assisting physicians in performing certain medical procedures and even giving shots, ouch. Skills are developed through a mix of gaining knowledge and experience.

Knowledge is having the theoretical or practical understanding of a subject. For example, a nurse needs to understand the fundamentals of medical care. A nurse assisting an eye doctor needs to know about vision, such as eye pressure and the purpose of various eye drops.

Experience is the practical knowledge or wisdom you gain from what you have observed, encountered, or undergone. This is a real-world test. I'm sure you've seen people with years of experience in a certain job. They make it look easy because they have done it so many times. Tom motioned to Susan and added, Susan was an actuarial analyst for thirty years. She could do work quickly and accurately with virtually no supervision. That's the kind of employee we all want!

We don't always think of relationships as part of a person's capabilities, even though for some jobs they may be the most important capability. As they say, "It's not what you know, it's who you know." Having the right contacts opens doors to getting things done. This is especially true in sales and raising capital.

Talent is a catch-all capability that essentially describes what we are good and bad at. Although the list is long, some of the characteristics of talent include IQ, disposition, energy level, extroversion, creativity, logic, empathy, self-awareness, expression, etc. These capabilities are hardwired into our brain and bodies and we can't do much to change them.

In business, each position requires a set of capabilities for success. Ryan and I talked about each of his direct reports. Both the needs of each position and brief analysis of how the respective individuals are meeting those needs. Ryan and I planned to use this time to put together a high-level action plan for him. I thought we'd capture some thoughts on paper. It will need tuning up once Ryan is back at work.

Tom flipped to a clean sheet of paper and wrote the word *LEADERSHIP* across the top of the page.

I believe any leader taking an organization through change needs an executive coach. A coach helps you hone in on specific areas to optimize your performance and uncover potential blind spots. Perhaps most importantly, they provide critical feedback others may fear to give you. For example, you may have a weak spot for a certain employee who is poisonous to the organization. Everybody knows you like them, and you send subtle messages you don't want to hear anything negative about them. A good coach will quickly hear about this person and help you see how you are hurting the company by not dealing with them.

You can engage an executive coach in a couple of ways: hire an individual or join a group. Top executive coaches can run over five hundred dollars an hour, but you don't need this. You are not running Apple—yet. You can probably find a good coach for around two hundred an hour. Initially, the coaching will be fairly heavy in terms of hours, but it will wind down as you create the needed change. You might spend twenty-five thousand per year for a couple of years.

My preference would be to join a coaching group. These organizations form CEO groups that are assigned a coach. The coach facilitates sessions where each CEO grapples with a problem. Since so many problems are shared at one point or another, everyone benefits. By the way, most problems relate to people.

Susan added, You belonged to that 10X CEO group that you really liked.

Good memory. That was many years ago. Yes, I was in a group with seven other CEOs that ran non-competing companies of a similar size. The feedback from the other CEOs was honest to the point of being brutal. I paid about thirty-five thousand per year to belong to this group, and it was the best money I ever spent.

Ryan said, OK, sounds like I have my first action item: find an executive coach.

Tom wrote under leadership **Engage Executive Coach**, then flipped to a new blank page and wrote *PEOPLE* across the top. Ryan and I discussed several action items related to his partners and direct reports. Do you remember them, Ryan?

Ryan grabbed the yellow pad and pen from Tom and wrote the following:

- **Me**—get executive coaching
- **Allie**—provide personal and technical support
- **Ed**—open conversation regarding his success and happiness in current role—evaluate whether he is in the right job and be prepared to make a change
- **David**—have a "come to Jesus meeting" and hopefully reengage him using the control model to give him more independence
- **Carol**—be mindful of her tendency to baby employees, especially as National moves to the control model with an emphasis on accountability.

Ryan asked, How's that, Tom?

I think that's a good summary. None of these will be one-and-done conversations. I think rolling out the control model will be a great forum to have these conversations. Also, the sooner you engage a coach, the better. They will help you navigate what will likely be some rough waters.

Cheryl touched Ryan's shoulder. Ryan, I hope you at least deal with David. I'm getting a little tired of hearing your complaints about him. I've always liked David, and he played a tremendous role in building the company to where it is. However, he doesn't seem to care as much as he once did.

Tom said, Ryan, I like how you used "moving to a control model" a couple of times. Sounds like you're serious about making some changes.

I am, Tom. I can see the effort this will require, but it makes too much sense to ignore. Don't worry, Cheryl, I will deal with David in the process.

Let's move to Community. Ryan, flip to a new page and write the purpose of National that you came up with.

Boy, let me think about that.

He then wrote the following on the new sheet: **PURPOSE: Ensuring that all animals have access to the medications they need to stay healthy.**

Tom gave a thumbs up. As we discussed, that is a rallying purpose for the animal lovers that are likely to join your company.

Values are fundamental beliefs that guide or motivate attitudes or actions. They help employees determine what is important to the organization. Having shared values builds the camaraderie required to effectively work together to achieve a common goal.

Ryan, do you remember the values you would like for National? Let's write them down.

Ryan was still holding the pen and wrote the following on the page underneath PURPOSE:

VALUES:

- **Follow the Golden Rule of treating people how you would like to be treated**
- **Always be trustworthy—do the right things the right way**
- **Move with a sense of urgency**

Tom said, To put it succinctly, maybe call them respect, trustworthiness, and sense of urgency?

Sure.

Tom asked Ryan to flip the legal pad back to the first page containing the control model schematic and pointed to the Strategy box. The third requirement of building a community is to have a strategic plan. A strategic plan has five core components: (1) a goal, (2) a description of the future state needed to achieve the goal, (3) a realistic assessment of the current state of affairs, (4) a list of action items needed to "fill the gap," and (5) a prioritization of those action items.

That sounds like an action item in and of itself, said Ryan.

I agree. The first step in creating a strategy is to have a strategic planning meeting with your executives. I suggest you have a pre-strategy meeting to agree on the purpose and values statements. These can then be used as guardrails in your strategy meeting.

I don't think I'd be comfortable self-facilitating either of these meetings, Ryan said. I assume we could get help?

Some executive coaches are willing and able to facilitate these types of meetings. Though I wouldn't make this a requirement, you can ask about it when you interview coaches. The most important aspect of a coach is your level of trust in them.

There are many consultants out there skilled in high-level meeting facilitation. I think their value is meeting preparation, organization, keeping the meeting on track and on time, and helping to follow up. If you're not going to follow up, don't waste your time!

Accountability, Ryan stated.

Yes, now you're getting ahead of Cheryl and Susan. We haven't discussed the Process muscle yet.

Tom snatched the yellow pad and pen from Ryan and wrote the following under the Values description.

PVS: Purpose, Values, Strategy

- **Hire meeting facilitator in next two weeks**
- **Schedule two-day executive meeting to craft company purpose and values statements within the next six weeks**
- **Schedule strategic planning meeting within four weeks of purpose and values meeting**

My schedule is filling up, said Ryan.

This is going to take discipline, Tom said. The fires will continue to come your way. This is your leadership challenge. Will you continue to do everyone else's job where you are both the control and choke points of the company? Or will you spend your time changing the company to one that is in control through its people, community, and processes?

Cheryl looked at Ryan. I hope you build this control model, Ryan. You need to get out of the wheel-spinning mode where you keep complaining about the same things over and over again.

You're right, Cheryl, but old habits are hard to break. Feel free to give me reminders.

I think you can count on that. Cheryl laughed.

Tom flipped back to the first page of the pad and pointed to the Process box. The third muscle group as we've already alluded to is Process. This is where the rubber hits the road. A company is an accumulation of its processes. When we talk about control, we are talking about processes being in control. Every process in an organization is there to achieve one or more objectives. For example, the logistics process at National is there to deliver needed medications on time to veterinarians or their clients.

However, processes do not operate in vacuums. They are interrelated and all support the achievement of the company's goals. Achieving National's logistics objective of delivering products on time would not ensure the company's overall goal is achieved if the products were not mixed correctly or the accounting department couldn't accurately bill and collect invoices. Everything must work together.

So, it's not enough to have great people that are clear on strategy and aligned to a common purpose and shared values. A company needs to have effective processes the people work in.

Tom pointed to the Control Framework and Policies and Procedures boxes and continued. For a company to be in control, or to have predictable outcomes that achieve goals and objectives, it must first create a control framework. Ryan and I talked about this in detail last night. There are four essential elements to having a strong control framework:

1. A commitment to integrity and ethical values
2. A clear Delegation of Authority
3. A Policy on Policies
4. A system that holds people accountable to agreed-upon objectives

The first starts with codifying your behavioral expectations in a Code of Conduct. A typical Code of Conduct requires employees to (1) abide by the law, (2) maintain a healthy and safe environment, (3) avoid conflicts of interest, (4) protect proprietary and confidential information, and (5) respect the property rights of others. The code is also where the purpose and values of the company are documented.

The formal Delegation of Authority is a written document that lays out what positions have what level of authority. The authority is typically described in financial terms. For example, an employee may be authorized to spend up to five hundred dollars without the boss's approval.

The Policy on Policies establishes processes and standards for developing, reviewing, and approving specific company policies. It also lists the core policies that the company will have. These can, of course, change, but you need a starting point.

Policies are important as they set behavioral expectations for employees in all the areas of the company. They also enable accountability and help defend against various types of legal claims.

Some typical policies a company should require include:

- Human resources
- Equal opportunity
- Substance abuse
- Workplace and cybersecurity
- Compensation

A system of accountability includes getting the people responsible for each process to achieve agreed-upon objectives. Successful completion of objectives is rewarded, and failing results in negative consequences. The key is the objectives must be agreed upon. Also, they should be specific, measurable, and time-based to minimize any vagueness that could put success into question.

Ryan and I discussed how critical accountability is to effective leadership. A leader can have almost any style or personality and be successful if they are clear about expected results and hold people accountable. And yelling and screaming at people that mess up is not holding them accountable. Instead, use consequences of reward and discipline.

Tom flipped the page to a new sheet. We need some action items for establishing a control framework. What do you suggest, Ryan?

Ryan took the pad and pen from Tom and, after thinking for a moment, wrote the following:

PROCESS

- **Becky to research codes of conduct and present recommendations**
- **Allie and Becky to work together to create a formal Delegation of Authority**
- **Management team to sit down and agree on what policies we need and create a Policy on Policies. Becky to lead in the development of policies themselves**
- **Strategic plan to address a system of accountability**

Good, said Tom. A couple of things, though. Each action item needs to be time-based. You will be putting in a lot of new controls that will take time. You can't do everything at once and will need to prioritize. I like your last bullet about addressing accountability in the strategic planning process. Maybe all of your action items from this weekend should flow through the strategic planning process since it ends with setting priorities.

It's a good thought, Tom. I'll consider that and, hopefully, have a coach to discuss it with soon.

Agreed. Finding the right coach is arguably your top priority.

Tom pivoted to address the group and said, Once you have established the control framework, you have an environment conducive to having effective processes.

Tom pointed at the Policies and Procedures box on the schematic. It is best to document your key processes in addition to having formal policies and procedures. Processes are different than policies. A process is a workflow, while a policy is guidance on expected behaviors for a set of circumstances such as travel. Documenting processes forces you to think about what you are doing, and oftentimes, you discover you are doing stupid stuff, for example, having two people sign checks under five hundred dollars. The risk of loss is too low to have a second person spend their time signing a multitude of small checks. Documented processes also support training new people and disciplining people who have not followed the proper procedures.

Cheryl broke in. I'll be honest with you; in all my years working, I've never seen a written policy and procedure or documented process.

Fair point, said Tom. First, it's possible they didn't have documented policies and procedures, or processes. Many small- and mid-sized companies don't. If you worked for a large publicly-traded company, I could assure you they had written procedures. These are more a tool for management versus a how-to manual for staff. You would have been likely trained by someone who was very familiar with the procedures and didn't feel the need to share the written documentation with you.

As processes flow, daily work gets done. There are typically built-in checks and balances that flag things going wrong. Sometimes they are immediate. For example, at National, if the logistics department ran out of shipping boxes, bells and sirens will immediately go off. However, if shipments go out incorrectly, the company will not know until customers complain.

The point is the business will run without documented processes. It will just run better with them. And in a competitive world, you need every advantage. Look at it as an opportunity. If documenting processes makes you a better company, and your competitors are not doing it, you can gain an advantage over them. Even if it's a slight cost advantage, this could mean more customers for you!

Susan said, Tom has an annoying saying that drove our kids crazy when they were growing up, "Life is about inches and seconds." He always said winning and losing come down to small differences. If you hesitate, you lose. If you don't fully stretch or jump your highest, you lose. He coached them in basketball and used it as a parallel for life.

Tom chuckled. I probably went too far with it, but I believe it. Excellent organizations, whether they are sports teams or businesses, have a sense of urgency that drives them to push as hard and fast as possible.

Ryan said, Having played a lot of sports and now running a business, I agree.

OK, let's wrap this up so we can all hit the road and get back home. Tom popped his knuckles. Chad, before we conclude, what do you think about all of this business talk?

It was kind of boring until the part about inches and seconds. Only when it comes to my video games, inches and seconds are too big. I wish I were a lot faster!

At least he'll have strong hands and wrists, Ryan said, laughing.

Tom chuckled. A control model is a system that a CEO relies on to ensure the company is under control. Control in this context means the company's goals and objectives are being predictably achieved. A control model for small companies is informal as the CEO can put their arms around the whole organization. In effect, by being personally involved in every meaningful decision.

As a company grows, a more formal control model is needed. The CEO loses the capacity to be involved in everything. They will eventually be making decisions other people should be making while becoming a bottleneck for decisions put on hold until the CEO has time. Both inches and seconds are lost. Maybe even miles and months!

The model we just discussed is not the only method for achieving control. None of the ideas are original, but the organization is one I've found that works. Before we say good-bye, let's page through Ryan's action items.

Tom turned to the first page schematic of the control model. The control model consists of three "muscle groups" that work together to form a strong corporate corpus. People. Community. Process. While PCP is the body of the company, leadership is the brain, and culture the soul.

Flipping to the People page, he said, Ryan has various conversations needing to take place with each of his executives. Some serious people issues will need to be resolved; however, people are complex, and these issues must be carefully addressed and given time.

Based on the action items, I suggest you add a conversation with Becky to ensure she feels she has the knowledge, skills, and talent to create the Code of Conduct and various policies that will need to be created.

Tom added to the page:

Ryan and Becky to discuss the new requirements for HR head

Makes sense, said Ryan.

Tom turned to the page with Purpose, Values, and Strategy action items. He said, A separate management meeting would be required to agree on the company's purpose and values. With these in hand, the management team would have its first strategy retreat to create goals and what it will take to achieve them. This includes setting priorities.

While flipping to the final Process page, Tom added, Also, each action item coming out of the Process muscle will be embedded into the strategic plan.

If this sounds easy, it is not. This is literally years of work. Setting priorities and having the discipline to stick with them will be extremely difficult. Also, the day-to-day fire drills will continue unabated until National is under control. However, in my experience, you will find things getting better far before everything is done. For example, you will see immediate positive changes just from these conversations with Ryan's direct reports.

Note we have not included documenting processes in Ryan's list of to-dos. You will need to agree on process objectives to create the system of accountability that drives results. However, this can be done without fully documenting the respective processes. The documentation will be a huge project that is more effectively done once the control framework is established. In my experience, by the time you get to documenting processes, you will feel it is not necessary. You still need to do it!

How are you feeling, Ryan? Tom asked.

I feel like I'm in better control just having a plan.

Did this make sense to you, Cheryl? Tom asked.

Yes, but I can see how difficult this will be for Ryan. It's just not how he's wired.

That's true of most entrepreneurs who have enjoyed Ryan's level of success. But those who make these changes generally enjoy better lives.

Tom handed the yellow pad to Ryan and said, Here you go, Ryan. This is rough, but a good start. Susan, let's grab the bags and head home.

They all shook hands and picked up their duffel bags and backpacks. They walked together to the porter. Tom's SUV was waiting in the drive as he had called in advance. As Tom opened the door to get in his car, he looked at Ryan.

Ryan, good luck to you. I wrote my email address and mobile phone number on the yellow pad in case you ever want to contact me. I'll be interested to hear how things go. Cheryl, you need to stay on top of him.

Ryan responded, I can't thank you enough. You were more than generous with your time this weekend. Susan, I'm sorry if I ruined your weekend. All this advice has meant so much to me.

He loves this stuff. I had a great time. Don't worry.

Tom said, You're welcome, Ryan. The best thing you could do for me is to implement the changes we discussed and let me know it all worked! I may not be as confident as I appear!

I suspect we will stay in touch. Have a safe ride back to Orange County.

The driveway pebbles crunched under the tires of Tom's dark gray SUV as it slowly accelerated out of the entrance of the Great Desert Resort & Spa. Tom and Susan appeared in a deep discussion as they headed for the freeway that would take them home. Ryan, Cheryl, and Chad watched them as they waited for their vehicle to be pulled up.

A LETTING GO LEADERSHIP CONTROL MODEL TEMPLATE

Creating and maintaining this template requires discipline and patience. The author has directly experienced putting this process in place at various organizations as a CEO and consultant. In all cases, he saw a dramatic improvement in the predictability of results. Please feel free to contact Dennis Drent at drentconsult.com to discuss your needs and ways in which he may be able to help.

XYZ Company

Letting Go Leadership—Current State Analysis

The purpose of this current state analysis is to measure the effectiveness of XYZ Company's Letting Go Leadership control model. The below template measures how XYZ is doing in each of the three core areas.

With your company, update this template at least quarterly and discuss it at management meetings. The results of these discussions should be action items that can be completed in the next ninety days to achieve both strategic and operational priorities.

People

The first section of the template is an exercise in evaluating the key people in the organization and should include no more than five individuals. The evaluation should be centered around the five key capabilities: Skills, Knowledge, Experience, Relationships, and Talent (SKERT).

Skills are the expertise needed to do a task and are developed through a mix of gaining knowledge and experience.

Knowledge is having the theoretical or practical understanding of a subject.

Experience is the practical knowledge or wisdom you gain from what you have observed, encountered, or undergone. This is a real-world test.

Relationships are critical. Having the right contacts opens doors to getting things done the right way.

Talent is a catch-all capability that essentially describes what we are good at. Although the list is long, some of the characteristics of talent include IQ, disposition, energy level, extroversion, creativity, logic, empathy, self-awareness, expression, etc.

Community

Community is made up of Purpose, Values, and Strategy, or PVS.

Purpose answers the basic question of why your business even exists and must be supplemented by a vision. The vision takes the purpose to a more aspirational level. To get the most out of employees, organizations need to offer more than a paycheck. People are more engaged if they believe in the purpose and vision of the organization they serve.

Values are fundamental beliefs that guide or motivate attitudes or actions. They help employees determine what is important to the organization. Having shared values builds the camaraderie required to effectively work together to achieve a common goal.

Strategy. A strategic plan has five core components:

- a goal
- description of future state needed to achieve the goal
- a realistic assessment of the current state of affairs
- a list of action items needed to fill the gap
- a prioritization of those action items.

The strategy is critical for communicating the priorities designed to achieve the company's high-level goals.

Process

Process is where the rubber hits the road. A company is an accumulation of its processes. Every process in an organization is there to achieve certain business objectives. They are in control when management knows the extent to which their objectives are being achieved. However, processes do not operate in vacuums. They are interdependent and must be looked at holistically.

How to use the assessments

The current state analysis is designed to assess the extent to which the organization is in control. Being in control does not mean goals and objectives are being achieved. Several factors outside any organizations' control may impact results. Being in control will reveal the extent to which goals and objectives are being achieved and what may be getting in the way. This enables action steps to stay or get back on course.

The current state assessment includes metrics and analysis required to evaluate all three muscle groups. Although intended to be comprehensive, each organization can tailor the assessment to fit its needs. To be effective, the assessment needs to be honest and lead to action.

People Assessment

In the SKERT section, check the box if they have a performance issue in that area. Otherwise, leave it blank.

	Overall Grade (A–F)	S	K	E	R	T	Description of performance issue and action required with associated time frame
CEO							
CFO							
CMO							
HR VP							
SVP Ops							

Community Assessment

	Company Statement	Change Needed (Yes/No)
Purpose		
Vision		
Values		

If change is needed, describe the action plan below.

	Description of needed change and action plan
Purpose	
Vision	
Values	

Business Model	Grade (A–F)	Description of competitive need to change the business model in any way
Business Model 1 (describe)		
Business Model 2 (describe)		

In the status section, red means it's not working at all, yellow means there are some problems with it, green means it is working well.

Strategy	Description	Status (Red/Yellow /Green)
Long-Term Goal		
Strategic Priority 1		
Strategic Priority 2		
Strategic Priority 3		

For any goal or initiative that is yellow or red, describe the deficiency below and associated corrective action with a time frame.

Strategy	Description of strategic deficiency and action plan with time frame
Long-Term Goal	
Strategic Priority 1	
Strategic Priority 2	
Strategic Priority 3	

Process Assessment

Control Framework	Grade (A–F)	Description of any needed updates, changes, or additions with time frames
Code of Conduct		
Delegation of Authority		
Policy on Policies		

Key Processes	Grade (A–F)	Description of any process deficiency preventing full achievement of process objectives
Process 1		
Process 2		
Process 3		
Process 4		
Process 5		

Key Process Improvement	Description of action items to eliminate process deficiencies preventing full achievement of process objectives, including a time frame
Process 1	
Process 2	
Process 3	
Process 4	
Process 5	

Accountability Metrics

Metric	1Q01	2Q01	3Q01	4Q01	1Q02	1Q02 vs. 1Q01
Revenue						
COGS						
Gross Profit						
Gross Margin						
OPEX						
EBITDA						
CAPEX						
Cash Flow						
Cash on Hand						
A/R						
A/R Past 90 Days						

Metric	1Q01	2Q01	3Q01	4Q01	1Q02	1Q02 vs. 1Q01
Current Ratio						
Debt Leverage (X.X Required)						
Fixed Charges Ratio (X.XX Required)						
Operating (e.g., orders filled on time)						
Marketing (e.g., website visits)						
Sales (e.g., online hit ratio)						
Customer Service (e.g., % calls answered in 20 seconds or less)						
Human Resources (e.g., employee turnover)						

ABOUT THE AUTHOR

Dennis Drent is an executive coach that offers forty years of trial and error know-how to managers that need to get better results. Dennis has an unusual mix of experience in moving from a background of auditing large public companies to being the CEO and COO of entrepreneurial mid-market companies later in his career. He has a track record of bringing control to underperforming organizations, enabling them to achieve desired results. This book condenses that experience into a control model applicable to any type of organization. Dennis lives with his wife Susan and dachshund Oscar in Yorba Linda, California, and can be reached by visiting drentconsult.com